SHORTEST HISTORY OF AI

Also in this series

The Shortest History of Europe by John Hirst
The Shortest History of England by James Hawes
The Shortest History of China by Linda Jaivin
The Shortest History of War by Gwynne Dyer
The Shortest History of Democracy by John Keane
The Shortest History of the Soviet Union by Sheila Fitzpatrick
The Shortest History of India by John Zubrzycki
The Shortest History of Greece by James Heneage
The Shortest History of the World by David Baker
The Shortest History of the Crown by Stephen Bates
The Shortest History of Economics by Andrew Leigh
The Shortest History of Italy by Ross King
The Shortest History of Japan by Lesley Downer
The Shortest History of Music by Andrew Ford
The Shortest History of Ancient Rome by Ross King
The Shortest History of France by Colin Jones
The Shortest History of Scandinavia by Mart Kuldkepp

THE SHORTEST HISTORY OF AI

TOBY WALSH

Black Inc.

Published by Black Inc.,
an imprint of Schwartz Books Pty Ltd
Wurundjeri Country
22–24 Northumberland Street
Collingwood VIC 3066, Australia
enquiries@blackincbooks.com
www.blackincbooks.com

Copyright © Toby Walsh 2025
Toby Walsh asserts his right to be known as the author of this work.

ALL RIGHTS RESERVED.
No part of this publication may be reproduced, stored in a retrieval system, or transmitted in any form by any means electronic, mechanical, photocopying, recording or otherwise without the prior consent of the publishers.

9781760645137 (paperback)
9781743823996 (ebook)

A catalogue record for this book is available from the National Library of Australia

Cover design and typesetting by Beau Lowenstern
Text design by Dennis Grauel
Cover image by DSGpro / iStock
Quote on p.1 from *The Hitchhiker's Guide to the Galaxy*, Douglas Adams, 1979

Printed in Australia by McPherson's Printing Group.

MIX
Paper | Supporting responsible forestry
FSC® C001695

Contents

How it begins   1

PART 1: THE SYMBOLIC ERA

Idea #1: Searching for answers   27

Idea #2: Making the best move   45

Idea #3: Following rules   61

INTERMISSION

The robots are coming   75

PART 2: THE LEARNING ERA

Idea #4: Artificial brains   95

Idea #5: Rewarding success   137

Idea #6: Reasoning about beliefs   159

PART 3: THE FUTURE

Achieving AI   175

Image credits   187
Acknowledgements   189
Notes   191
Index   195

For Andrea

PREHISTORY		1837 Analytical Engine	First mechanical computer. Designed by Charles Babbage but never completed.
		1843 Creativity	Ada Lovelace asks if computers would ever be creative.
		1940 Nimatron	First AI game. Unveiled at the World's Fair in New York.
		1943 Neural network	First neural network. Proposed by Walter Pitts and Warren McCulloch.
		1948 Turochamp	First chess computer. Invented by Alan Turing and David Champernowne.
		1949 ELMER and ELSIE	First primitive robots. Built by William Grey Walter in Bristol.
		1950 Turing Test	First scientific paper on AI. Alan Turing proposes test to determine when AI has succeeded.
		1955 Logic Theorist	An artificial mathematician. Often called the first AI program. It wasn't.
SYMBOLIC ERA		1956 Unofficial start of AI	First meeting on AI, held at Dartmouth College. The term "artificial intelligence" coined by John McCarthy to secure funding for meeting.
		1957 Mark 1 Perceptron	First neural network implemented by Frank Rosenblatt.
		1960 MENACE	Matchbox computer invented by Donald Michie at Edinburgh. Learns to play noughts and crosses perfectly.
		1964 ELIZA	First chatbot. Designed by Joseph Weizenbaum at MIT.
		1965 DENDRAL	First expert system. Developed at Stanford University.
		1968	Arthur C. Clarke predicts that machines will match or exceed human intelligence by 2001.
		1969 A* search	AI algorithm invented at Stanford Research Institute to navigate Shakey the robot.
		1969 Perceptrons	Critical book ends much research into neural networks.
		1971 STRIPS	AI planning algorithm invented to solve goals for Shakey the robot.
		1973 AI winter	Sir James Lighthill's report about the lack of progress and prospects for AI precipitates the first AI winter.
		1979 BKG 9.8	First world champion loses to an AI when Luigi Villa is beaten in a backgammon match.

SYMBOLIC ERA (*CONT*)	1982 AI Spring	Japan's ambitious Fifth Generation Systems program heralds the start of an AI spring.
	1986 SLAM	Simultaneous localisation and mapping method invented to enable a robot to map and locate in its environment.
	1987 AI winter	Expert system boom collapses, starting the second AI winter.
	1994 Prometheus	European self-driving car project. Two cars developed drive over 1000 km around Paris at speeds reaching 130 kmph.
	1997 IBM Deep Blue	Garry Kasparov becomes the first world chess champion to lose to a computer.
	2001	Machines have not matched human intelligence.
	2002 Roomba	iRobot's vacuum cleaner, and now the world's most popular robot, launched.
	2005 Stanley	Stanford's self-driving car wins the 2nd DARPA Prize by driving across 132 miles of the Mojave Desert.
	2007 Chinook	AI program proved to play checkers "perfectly". It never loses.
	2007 ImageNet	Image recognition dataset launched by Fei-Fei Li. Reinvigorates research into neural networks.
	2011 IBM Watson	AI wins at *Jeopardy!* against two of the best human players ever to have played the general knowledge quiz.
LEARNING ERA	2012 AlexNet	Deep learning neural network convincingly wins annual ImageNet competition. Heralds the start of the second AI Spring.
	2015 OpenAI	Elon Musk, Sam Altman and others found the not-for-profit company OpenAI.
	2016 AlphaGo	DeepMind's AlphaGo beats world Go champion Lee Sedol.
	2017 Libratus	Professional poker players beaten for the first time by an AI program.
	2017 Transformer	Team at Google Research propose transformer neural network. This is the "T" in ChatGPT.
GENERATIVE AI ERA	2022 ChatGPT	OpenAI launches ChatGPT. It gains a million users in the first week.
	2023 AlphaFold	DeepMind's AlphaFold predicts shape of nearly every protein known to science.
	2024 AI Nobel Prizes	Physics Nobel awarded to Geoffrey Hinton and John Hopfield for neural networks; Chemistry Nobel to Demis Hassabis and John Jumper for AlphaFold.
FUTURE	2062 AGI	The 2018 book by author titled 2062: *The World that AI Made*, which predicts machines will have matched human intelligence by 2062, is finally proven wrong.

HOW IT BEGINS

ARTIFICIAL INTELLIGENCE BEGAN on 18 June 1956. It was a Monday.

18 June is International Panic Day, which seems appropriate for the day humanity started working on AI. It's a day on which it's recommended you ignore author Douglas Adams' famous advice:

> In many of the more relaxed civilizations on the Outer Eastern Rim of the Galaxy, the *Hitchhiker's Guide* has already supplanted the great *Encyclopaedia Galactica* as the standard repository of all knowledge and wisdom ... [I]t scores over the older, more pedestrian work in two important respects.
>
> First, it is slightly cheaper; and secondly it has the words *DON'T PANIC* inscribed in large friendly letters on its cover.

Another author, Arthur C. Clarke, suggested that "Don't panic" was perhaps the best advice that could be given to the human race. And in 2018, SpaceX launched Elon Musk's old Tesla Roadster into space with the words "DON'T PANIC" written on the dashboard.

Now, you might be surprised that AI began all the way back in the 1950s. It seems a distant time. And it is easy to be nostalgic about that period. The civil rights movement was taking off. The postwar world was enjoying a period of economic recovery and stability. And "Heartbreak Hotel" was topping the charts. As I said, this was quite a long time ago. 1956 might well be before you were born? It's before I was born. And I've been dreaming about AI for most of my life – well, ever since I was a young boy reading too much science fiction. Back then I read authors like Arthur C. Clarke and Isaac Asimov who wrote about a future of robots and intelligent computers. That future now seems to be arriving.

When the AI chatbot ChatGPT was launched at the end of 2022, it appeared to have come out of nowhere. You couldn't open a newspaper without reading multiple articles about AI. Many of us started to be concerned. Even governments began to panic. Where was this all going to end?

But the reality was that AI's overnight success was, like most overnight successes, a long time in the making. Indeed, as you'll find out later in this book, AI has been part of your life for decades. It's just that many of the other examples of AI in your life before ChatGPT weren't perhaps as visible.

You might also be surprised that AI has a particular day on which it starts. Most scientific disciplines don't start on a specific date. Artificial intelligence is different. Monday, 18 June 1956 was the first day of an eight-week-long workshop whose goal was to build intelligent machines. And the meeting marked the start of the field of artificial intelligence.

The workshop was held on the leafy campus of Dartmouth College, an Ivy League school in the pretty town of Hanover, New Hampshire. The college was founded in 1769 to educate Native Americans in Christian theology and the English way of life. By 1956, however, Dartmouth had largely forgotten the cause of Native Americans, Christian theology and the English way of life and had evolved into one of the most prestigious and selective undergraduate colleges in the United States. Indeed, it was so "selective" that the college wouldn't admit female undergraduates till over a dozen years later, in 1972. The 1956 workshop was itself an all-male affair. And sadly, women are still poorly represented in AI today. It's a problem that ought to be fixed but, despite many efforts, doesn't seem to be going away.

The Dartmouth workshop was organised by John McCarthy, a young assistant professor at the college with an ambitious dream. His dream was ancient – to build a machine that could think. He therefore invited a group of likeminded colleagues from the United States, Canada and the United Kingdom to New Hampshire to join him in building an artificially intelligent future.

In 1956, computers were just starting to become widely available. IBM had introduced the legendary IBM 650 mainframe computer in late 1954. It was the first mass-produced computer. Indeed, the IBM 650 would prove to be the most popular computer of the 1950s and the first computer to turn a profit. 1956 was therefore a suitable moment to consider how

A young John McCarthy.

far we could push these digital beasts. Could they perhaps one day think? It was a bold question to ask, but John McCarthy was anything but shy.

John McCarthy would go on to found the legendary AI Lab at Stanford University in 1962. This lab is famous for a number of AI breakthroughs. In 2005, for example, the lab gave us Stanley, a self-driving car that won the US$2 million DARPA challenge by driving across 132 miles of the Mojave Desert (around 212 kilometres) without a human driver. The lab also gave us a little-known company founded in 1996 that used AI to search the web. That company was called BackRub. In 1997, the founders decided the name was a bit of a mistake, and renamed the company Google.

> Google was perhaps a better name than BackRub but it was another mistake. It's a misspelling of googol, an astronomically large number loved by physicists. A googol is 10^{100}, which is an insanely large number. In longhand it is 10,000,000,000,000,000,000,000,000,000,000,000,000,000,000,000,000,000,000,000,000,000,000,000,000,000,000,000,000,000,000,000,000,000,000,000,000,000,000,000,000,000,000,000,000,000. This is 1 followed by 100 zeroes. This is way more than the number of atoms in the universe (currently estimated to be around 10^{80}). In fact, a googol is more bytes than Google or indeed any company will ever index without violating the laws of physics. Google has presently indexed only around 10^{17} bytes of data. But over-promising doesn't seem to be considered much of a problem in Silicon Valley.

I was lucky enough to know John McCarthy. This is not as impressive as it may sound: AI is a surprisingly small field. The Stanford AI Index records that annually fewer than 100 PhDs in AI graduate and stay in academic research in the United States and Canada.[1] It is therefore not that difficult to know one of the founding figures. Indeed, I not only knew John McCarthy, I very nearly drowned him in Sydney Harbour one Sunday afternoon in 2006. But that's a story for a longer history.*

---

* If you want to read the story of how I nearly became a footnote in the history of AI by almost drowning John McCarthy, you'll need to read my first book, *It's Alive! Artificial Intelligence from the Logic Piano to Killer Robots*.

McCarthy had a formidable intellect and strong political views. He is most famous for coining the term "artificial intelligence". He came up with the name to describe the topic of that Dartmouth meeting in 1956. Artificial intelligence was quickly shortened to AI, a two-letter acronym that perhaps resonates with other two-letter acronyms about intelligence involving a vowel like IQ and EQ.

Artificial intelligence was a sufficiently provocative idea for 1956 to get US$7500 towards the cost of the workshop from the Rockefeller Foundation, a philanthropic organisation with the mission of promoting the wellbeing of humanity by advancing science and innovation. (Perhaps the Rockefeller Foundation wasn't fully convinced about AI's prospects of promoting humanity's wellbeing, as the proposal had actually asked for $13,500, nearly twice as much.) The proposal to hold the meeting suggested that:

> Every aspect of learning or any other feature of intelligence can in principle be so precisely described that a machine can be made to simulate it. An attempt will be made to find how to make machines use language, form abstractions and concepts, solve kinds of problems now reserved for humans, and improve themselves.

If that wasn't ambitious enough, the proposal also made a brave prediction on how long it would take: "We think that a significant advance can be made in one or more of these problems if a carefully selected group of scientists work on it together for a summer." This proved somewhat optimistic.

Indeed, many critics argue that AI has been over-promising and under-delivering ever since.

As you will have surmised, the eight-week workshop at Dartmouth didn't make a significant advance on building AI. Getting machines to think proved to be a much greater scientific challenge than McCarthy or his colleagues imagined. Indeed, this book is a short history of our efforts to do what these pioneers tried, and failed, to do that summer. The workshop did, however, put AI on the map. Perhaps its most significant outcomes were two simple but immensely powerful approaches to building AI. The first was to build AI using symbols. And the second was to build AI using learning. These two approaches define the two main eras of AI: the era of symbolic systems, which ran till the 1990s, and the era of machine learning that followed, and that is now causing much of the AI hype.

This short history is therefore divided into two parts. In the first part, I explore the early, symbolic era of artificial intelligence. This is a time in which computers conquered chess and many other human games. But it was also a time of frustration, when we discovered how hard it was going to be to move beyond simple games and build AI. This should be reassuring. Intelligence is complex. Building it in silicon hasn't proved easy. In the second part of this history, I explore the more recent learning era of artificial intelligence. We stopped trying to program AI ourselves and instead got computers to learn to do intelligent stuff themselves. Just like you *learnt* to do most of the intelligent tasks you can now do, computers have now learnt to read, write and do mathematics. This brings us up to today and recent successes like the AI chatbot ChatGPT, which learnt to read a large part of the internet.

The book concludes, rather unusually for a history, by looking at the future. The history of artificial intelligence is far from complete. What happens when we actually succeed in building machines that think? How long will this take? And might AI be an existential threat to humanity?

This history is also unusual in another respect. Histories are usually about extraordinary people and groundbreaking events. This history is not. It is the story of just six ideas. That's it. Six ideas. All you need to know to understand artificial intelligence today are these six ideas. Each idea will get its own chapter. And to give you a proper understanding of AI, I won't shy away from somewhat technical descriptions. This will reveal that there is a lot less magic to AI than the media would have you believe.

Of course, you'll also meet some remarkable people along the way, such as the aforementioned John McCarthy, and the person on the UK's 50-pound note, the even more remarkable Alan Turing. And you'll hear about some groundbreaking moments, such as when AI got better than humans and claimed its first world championship.

Before I start, let me repeat a warning from Arthur Samuel. Samuel was one of the attendees of the Dartmouth meeting in 1956, and the author of a breakthrough AI program for the game of checkers that was one of the first demonstrations of the power of machine learning. In 1962, he wrote:

As always, with any revolution, there is a lunatic fringe – people who believe in magic, or those who are carried away with their enthusiasm for a new cause and who make wild claims which tend to discredit the entire undertaking. The field of artificial intelligence has, perhaps, had more than its share of these people ... Nevertheless, it seems certain that the time is not far distant when most of the more humdrum mental tasks, which now take so much human time, will be done by machine. Artificial intelligence is neither a myth nor a threat to man.[2]

Let me therefore help you cut through the lunacy, the wild claims, the myths and the threats about AI with this rather personal and short history of AI.

> **AI IN THE MOVIES**
>
> The silver screen has driven both the perception and the construction of AI. OpenAI, for example, tried unsuccessfully to license Scarlett Johansson's voice to be the interface to ChatGPT, just as she voiced Samantha, the voice of the AI operating system in the 2013 movie *Her*. Here are some other famous examples of AI from the movies.
>
> **METROPOLIS (1927)**: Fritz Lang's classic is one of the first feature-length science fiction films ever made. Maschinenmensch, the machine-human at the centre of this movie, is a humanoid robot designed by the mad scientist Rotwang to impersonate Maria, a beloved figure among the oppressed workers in the dystopian city of Metropolis.

FORBIDDEN PLANET (1956): In this classic science fiction film, Robby the Robot is a highly advanced, autonomous and friendly mechanical servant. Robby makes guest appearances in a number of TV series, including *The Addams Family*, where he appears as Smiley in the 1966 episode "Lurch's Little Helper".

BLADE RUNNER (1982): The replicants in *Blade Runner* are bioengineered AI-powered robots designed by the Tyrell Corporation to be virtually identical to humans and used for off-world labour. Replicants possess enhanced strength, agility and, in some cases, intelligence. However, they have a limited lifespan of four years to prevent them from developing emotions and self-awareness. Replicant Roy Batty, played by Rutger Hauer in his most famous role, gives one of the most moving and well-known death soliloquies in movie history: "I've seen things you people wouldn't believe ... Attack ships on fire off the shoulder of Orion ... I watched C-beams glitter in the dark near the Tannhäuser Gate. All those moments will be lost in time, like tears in rain ... Time to die."

THE TERMINATOR (1984): In this movie, an AI defence network called Skynet becomes self-aware and perceives humans as a threat to its existence. To protect itself, Skynet launches a nuclear holocaust known as Judgement Day. Skynet sends a Terminator, a nearly indestructible cyborg, back in time to kill Sarah Connor and prevent her giving birth to the leader of the human resistance. In the early 2000s, China started developing a massive surveillance network called Skynet. According to the Chinese newspaper *People's Daily*, Skynet can scan the faces of over 1 billion people in one second.

EX MACHINA (2014): Ava in this movie is a highly advanced humanoid robot capable of complex thought, emotion and possibly even self-awareness. Ava's realistic appearance and behaviour blur the line between human and machine. Murray Shanahan, a professor of cognitive robotics at Imperial College and senior scientist at DeepMind was a consultant on the movie.

TRANSCENDENCE (2014): After being mortally wounded by techno terrorists, the consciousness of AI researcher Dr Will Casteris is uploaded into a supercomputer by his wife and friend. As this AI begins to expand its capabilities, it transforms society but also raises fears of uncontrolled power. Elon Musk makes a brief appearance in the movie as an extra. He co-founded the AI company OpenAI one year later.

MISSION IMPOSSIBLE: DEAD RECKONING (2023): A rogue AI called "the Entity" threatens global security. Originally an advanced US cyber weapon, the AI gains sentience and outsmarts its creators, manipulating defence systems and financial networks at will. Ethan Hunt and his IMF team race to destroy the Entity, but it proves to be a formidable foe, hacking communications and impersonating humans with ease.

AI'S PREHISTORY

While the Dartmouth workshop in 1956 is the official birthplace of AI, it wasn't the first time that people had thought about building thinking machines. However, without access to computers, there wasn't much you could do before 1956 to advance those dreams. That was unless you were an exceptional thinker.

Perhaps the most exceptional mind to think about thinking machines before 1956 was the British mathematician Alan Turing. *Time* magazine named Turing one of the 100 most important people of the twentieth century. He, more than anyone, is responsible for the digital age in which we now live.*

During the Second World War, Alan Turing helped build one of the first practical computing devices, the beautifully named Bombe. This was used to crack the German Enigma military codes, a mathematical feat that likely shortened the war by at least two years, saving millions of lives. In 1936, before these codebreaking exploits and before anyone on the planet had *actually* built an electronic computer, Alan Turing came up with an abstract mathematical model of a computer. This model is simple but immensely powerful. It describes, for example, everything from your smartphone to the fastest supercomputer.

Turing wanted to answer a simple question. What can a machine compute? Can it, for example, prove complex mathematical results like Fermat's Last Theorem? Or write a beautiful sonnet about falling in love? If we're going to get

---

* Sadly, Alan Turing died before I was born so I never had the chance to meet him. However, AI is a small field so I (like many others) share an academic connection. Turing studied at Cambridge University under Ludwig Wittgenstein. One of Wittgenstein's other PhD students was the mathematician Reuben Goodstein, famous for Goodstein's theorem. And one of Goodstein's PhD students was Alan Bundy, who became a professor in the department of artificial intelligence at Edinburgh University and, in time, my PhD supervisor.

"This is only a foretaste of what is to come and only the shadow of what is going to be": Alan Turing quoted on the British 50-pound note.

machines to think, he reasoned, it would be good to know their limits. Turing came up with a deceptively simple and tautological-sounding answer to this question: a machine can compute anything that his mathematical model of a computer can. And, by extension, if something cannot be computed by his mathematical model, then making the computer bigger or faster won't help. Turing's mathematical model of a computer is now called a "Turing machine". And, for good measure, Turing also identified a number of problems that a Turing machine, and therefore even today's fastest supercomputer, *cannot* compute. For instance, you'd like to know that a flight control system in an aeroplane can never stop. But this is the sort of problem that Turing identified as impossible in general to compute.

This is mind-blowing. Before we physically had the first electronic computer, Alan Turing had worked out the fundamental limits of what it, and indeed every computer that has followed, could possibly compute. It's like one of the Wright brothers predicting the barrier that the speed of sound would present to faster flight before Orville Wright had even made that first flight over the sand dunes of Kitty Hawk, North Carolina. Now, before you dismiss this book as the history of an impossible dream, Turing's limits of what you can and cannot compute did not include artificial intelligence. His results left open the possibility of AI, the possibility that we might reduce thinking to computation.

Turing's findings about the limits of computers would be enough to earn him a spot in a history book about AI. But his contributions go well beyond identifying these limits. In 1950, Alan Turing wrote what is generally considered the first scientific paper about AI. It begins, "I propose to consider the question, 'Can machines think?'"[3] He had already provided a good definition of the word "machine" back in 1936. But that still left the problem of what the word "think" means. Turing proposed to side-step this definitional problem with an ingenious idea. He called it the "imitation game", but it is now more commonly called the "Turing test". If a person remotely conversing with a machine and a human cannot tell them apart, then might we not say that the machine thinks?

The Turing test has its critics. Should we really be building machines that try to deceive us into thinking that they're human? What questions distinguish man from machine? And, since a machine cannot experience the world like a human being, is it even a fair test? If the machine fails, does that truly mean it cannot think? Despite such concerns, the Turing test gives you a good idea of what AI researchers like me are trying to do. We're trying to get computers to do the sorts of things that humans do that we believe require thinking. This covers sensing, reasoning and acting. Making sense of what we see and hear. Reasoning about we see and hear. Then making plans, and acting on those plans. All of these require intelligence. And so, getting a robot to sense, reason and act in the world requires artificial intelligence.

Alan Turing was thus the genius who helped start the field of AI. Sadly, he died two years before the Dartmouth workshop. He was just 41 years old. A half-eaten apple lay beside his bed and an inquest later determined that cyanide poisoning was the cause of his untimely death. In 2009, the UK prime minister, Gordon Brown, apologised for Turing's prosecution for "homosexual acts", which many believe led to him lacing that apple with cyanide.

Of course, Turing isn't the only exceptional person who thought about AI before computers became commonplace. Some others deserve a mention too. Ada Lovelace is one such person. Ada was the daughter of the poet Lord Byron. And, like Alan Turing, she died tragically young, at just 36. She worked with Charles Babbage on his mechanical computer, the Analytical Engine. Babbage was a Victorian polymath, mathematician, inventor, mechanical engineer and aspiring politician. You can see half of his brain in the Science Museum in London. Oddly, the other half is 6 kilometres away, in the Hunterian Museum at the Royal College of Surgeons. Babbage had a simple but important ambition: to reduce the errors in the mathematical tables used for navigation and artillery. And so, he turned to the most cutting-edge technology of Queen Victoria's era, mechanical gears and the punched cards of the Jacquard loom, to design a programmable computer that could compute such tables without error.

Babbage's Analytical Engine had many parts found in modern-day computers. It had memory in which to store data, a logic unit that could do arithmetic and even a printer on which to produce output. It was a remarkable device that could read in and execute different programs. Babbage memorably described it as being able to "eat its own tail", like "a locomotive that lays down its own railway". Unfortunately, the Analytical Engine was never finished. If it had been, it would have been a Turing machine, able to compute anything today's fastest supercomputer could – just slower. It's worth imagining how such a mechanical beast might have transformed Victorian Britain.

The remarkable Ada Lovelace.

Ada Lovelace was clearly captivated by the possibility of what Babbage's marvellous Analytical Engine might do. And she, in turn, captivated the older Charles Babbage. He called her "the Enchantress of Number", but I suspect it was not just numbers that she enchanted.

To demonstrate the Analytical Engine's potential, Lovelace wrote the world's first complex computer program. It was a set of instructions to calculate Bernoulli numbers. The first computer programmer was thus a woman. As were many of the first "computers" – humans who performed complex astronomical and other calculations before one of Turing's machines took over such arduous tasks.

> Bernoulli numbers are an important sequence of numbers that have many applications in mathematics, such as in approximating the tangent function. The sequence begins 1, 1/2, 1/6, 0, -1/30, 0, 1/42, 0, -1/30, 0, 5/66, 0, -691/2730, 0, 7/6, 0, -3617/510 and continues for ever.

However, Lovelace had more ambitious dreams for the Analytical Engine than just calculating Bernoulli numbers. She wrote:

> [I]t might act upon other things besides number ... Supposing, for instance, that the fundamental relations of pitched sounds in the science of harmony and of musical composition were susceptible of such expression and adaptations, the engine might compose elaborate and

scientific pieces of music of any degree of complexity or extent ... We may say most aptly that the Analytical Engine weaves algebraic patterns, just as the Jacquard loom weaves flowers and leaves.[4]

Holy moly! Where did this come from? Babbage was interested in calculating tables of numbers. But Lovelace somehow looked forwards over a century to a time when computers would manipulate sounds, images, videos and many other things besides numbers. Your smartphone is, at the end of the day, a small computer. And it is so versatile because it manipulates not just numbers but also sounds, images and videos. It is thus part music player, part camera, part video recorder and part game engine.

Despite Lovelace's idea that computers could do more than just calculate numbers, she was also one of the first critics of artificial intelligence. Indeed, she was quick to dismiss the dream of building machines that would be creative: "The Analytical Engine has no pretensions whatever to originate anything," she said. "It can do whatever we know how to order it to perform. It can follow analysis, but it has no power of anticipating any analytical relations or truths."[5] Lovelace's complaint has haunted the field of AI ever since. Computers just do what we tell them to do. They lack that human spark of creativity. It's a criticism of AI that we will test multiple times during this history.

There are many other extraordinary characters besides Alan Turing, Charles Babbage and Ada Lovelace to meet in even the shortest history of AI. We should, of course, meet

George Boole, a self-taught English mathematician from Lincoln who became the first professor of mathematics at Queen's College, Cork.* In 1847, Boole invented Boolean logic, the logic of 0s and 1s that powers modern-day computers. He would die at just 49 years old after his wife, Mary Everest, threw buckets of cold water over him as he lay in bed. We should also meet Gottfried Wilhelm Leibniz, a polymath from Leipzig and a contemporary of Isaac Newton. He took time out from arguing with Newton about who invented calculus to imagine an "alphabet of human thought". He proposed to represent each fundamental concept by a unique symbol, and to reduce thought to calculation.

> Mary Everest was niece to George Everest, surveyor and geographer after whom the mountain was named. She was a homeopath who believed in curing like with like. And George Boole had caught a cold in the rain. Thanks to Mary's buckets of water, Boole's cold turned into pneumonia, and then death.

And we should meet Thomas Hobbes, an English philosopher who was tutor to Prince Charles, later King Charles II.

---

* Queen's College would become University College Cork in 1908. When I worked at University College Cork, I would think of Boole every time I cycled past 5 Grenville Place and saw the bronze plaque which recorded where Boole lived and wrote his masterpiece, *An Investigation of the Laws of Thought*.

Unlike many of the characters so far, Hobbes didn't die an untimely death but lived to 91, a considerable age for the 16th century. He, too, imagined reducing thinking to computing:

> By reasoning, I understand computation. And to compute is to collect the sum of many things added together at the same time, or to know the remainder when one thing has been taken from another. To reason therefore is the same as to add or to subtract.[6]

This was remarkably prescient. Three hundred years before Alan Turing helped design and build one of the first electronic computers, Hobbes had the idea that thinking might be reduced to mere computation. And let us not forget the 13th-century Catalan writer, poet, theologian, mystic and mathematician Ramon Llull. Llull invented a primitive logic which could be mechanically used to identify what he claimed were all possible truths about a subject. As you might be expecting by now, Llull met an untimely end. He was stoned to death by a Muslim crowd he was, one can suppose unsuccessfully, trying to convert to Christianity. But I'm afraid in this shortest history I don't have the space to dwell further on any of these exceptional minds and untimely deaths.

ANCIENT DREAMS
Despite what I've told you so far, the history of AI doesn't actually begin with Lovelace, Leibniz or Llull. It starts much earlier, in the mists of antiquity, with mythical stories of artificial beings endowed with intelligence and consciousness.

Beings like Talos and the Golem that have haunted humanity.

In Greek mythology, Talos is a living bronze sculpture given to Minos to guard the island of Crete. Talos was forged by Hephaestus, the god of fire. Today, Talos has morphed into an even more worrying creation, a crypto exchange. In Jewish mythology, Golems are human-like figures created from clay or mud and animated with life. One of the most famous, the Golem of Prague, was created to defend the Prague ghetto from pogroms and other antisemitic attacks. Golems are obedient and powerful. You might think of them, therefore, as low-tech robots. And in many of the stories, like the Golem of Prague, the Golem either follows instructions too literally or goes AWOL, wreaking havoc upon its human creators. The Golem thus taps into our deeply rooted anxiety and fascination with our inventions getting out of control. This is, of course, a theme that Mary Shelley famously explored in her 1818 literary masterpiece, *Frankenstein, or the Modern Prometheus*.

While Shelley's novel is arguably the first true piece of science fiction, it looks back to these ancient myths as much as it looks forwards. Don't forget that the Creature threatens to kill Victor Frankenstein's friends and loved ones and not stop until he has completely ruined him. Victor himself dies before he has hunted down and killed the Creature in revenge for his father's death.

As its title suggests, Shelley's book is about the Promethean fear that has long haunted humanity. Prometheus was the crafty Titan who gave humans fire and had his liver pecked out daily for his transgression. His story sparks the fear that playing with divine gifts might just burn us all. Technology often

The visionary Mary Shelley.

brings unintended and undesirable consequences. Fire gave us warmth and cooking. But it also gave us war and destruction. The internal combustion engine gave us mobility and industry. But it is now giving us climate change. Splitting the atom gave us cheap and green power but also the nuclear bomb. And now the computer is giving us artificial intelligence. What might be the unintended and undesirable consequences?

There are many obvious risks. Will our economies struggle to cope with massive unemployment and income inequality? Will democracies sink under a sea of misinformation and disinformation? Will warfare be transformed terribly by killer robots? It's easy to imagine a host of negative outcomes.

Of course, there is also a large upside to artificial intelligence. Indeed, AI is already doing much to improve your life. It is discovering new drugs. Halicin, the latest antibiotic, was not discovered using human intellect but with AI. It's named after HAL, the AI in *2001: A Space Odyssey*. Artificial intelligence also now detects early signs of Alzheimer's disease from brain scans, efficiently and effectively identifies credit card fraud, schedules preventive maintenance before ageing water pipes fail and saves lives by predicting the paths of cyclones.

But the quest for artificial intelligence is a much more profound story than one of building technology to improve our lives. It is as much a story about ourselves as it is about technology. It asks two fundamental questions that go to the core of our existence.

What is special about human intelligence?
And might we tame and build it in silicon?

As for the answers to these two profound questions, only history will tell.

PART 1
THE SYMBOLIC ERA

IDEA #1:

SEARCHING FOR ANSWERS

AI BEGINS WITH THE symbolic era. This starts at Dartmouth in 1956 and runs through to the 1990s, when the learning era takes hold. The roots of the symbolic era can, however, be traced back before 1956, past Alan Turing and Ada Lovelace, all the way to ancient Greek, Chinese, Indian and Islamic cultures.

Aristotle, for example, developed one of the first *symbolic logics*, in Athens in the third century BC. Indeed, you were likely first exposed to the concept of logic via his famous syllogism: *All men are mortal. Socrates is a man. Therefore, Socrates is mortal.** Here "man", "mortal" and "Socrates" are symbols. They represent the concept of a man, the property of being mortal and the person Socrates respectively. I could replace these symbols with different symbols, such as "bear", "brown" and "Knut". These represent instead the concept of a bear, the property of being brown and a famous polar bear named

---

* I apologise for the sexism in this example. Women are also mortal. Indeed, our mortal existence depends critically on women!

Knut. Aristotle's famous syllogism then becomes: *All bears are brown. Knut is a bear. Therefore, Knut is brown.* Of course, having stated that all bears are brown, I can derive problematic conclusions about white polar bears like Knut. But such problems aside, it's not hard to see that computers can easily manipulate symbols like this. And symbols are thus central to having computers reason, not just calculate.

Knut in 2007 on his debut at Berlin Zoo.

It's easy to be blinded by Western chauvinism and overlook important contributions from other parts of the globe. For instance, two centuries before Aristotle, we find syllogisms in the *Nyāya Sūtras*, an ancient Indian Sanskrit text. And the Logicians were, as their name might suggest, a school of philosophers interested in logical argument around the same time as Aristotle, but far away from Athens in the Zhou dynasty in China.

IDEA #1: SEARCHING FOR ANSWERS

Symbols, then, are fundamental to AI. This should not be surprising. Intelligence is connected to language. Is language not the stuff of thought? And language itself is just a bunch of symbols. Indeed, symbols set up one of the most fundamental problems facing AI, the so called "symbol grounding" problem. How do we "ground" or connect symbols in a computer with what they represent in the real world? How, for example, do we connect the word "Socrates" with the ancient Greek philosopher called Socrates? Or the word "Knut" with the (sadly now deceased) polar bear named Knut? The well-known American philosopher and AI sceptic John Searle identified this problem in his celebrated "Chinese room" argument:

> Imagine a native English speaker who knows no Chinese locked in a room full of boxes of Chinese symbols (a data base) together with a book of instructions for manipulating the symbols (the program). Imagine that people outside the room send in other Chinese symbols which, unknown to the person in the room, are questions in Chinese (the input). And imagine that by following the instructions in the program the man in the room is able to pass out Chinese symbols which are correct answers to the questions (the output). The program enables the person in the room to pass the Turing Test for understanding Chinese but he does not understand a word of Chinese.[1]

Searle's Chinese room is an argument against a computer having a "mind", "understanding" and perhaps "consciousness". Fortunately, his argument leaves open the idea of AI. Such a Chinese room might, as Searle himself postulates, exist. Its existence wouldn't violate any laws of physics, as far as we are aware – even if we might struggle to connect the symbols in the Chinese room with the associated concepts in the outside world. An AI program could, like the Chinese room, answer Chinese questions intelligently – without understanding the symbols or grounding them in reality.

This idea – representing concepts in the wider world with symbols – is one that we all use daily. For example, we happily represent whole countries by two-digit numbers. Australia by 61. Belgium by 32. China by 86. Denmark by 45. Egypt by 20. France by 33. As you may have worked out, these are dial codes. The telephone network is nothing more than a vast distributed computer that uses these mathematical symbols to route calls. In aviation, three-letter symbols represent airports. SYD for Kingsford Smith Airport in Sydney. JFK for John F. Kennedy International Airport in New York. PEK for Beijing International Airport. And LHR for Heathrow Airport in London. Symbols connect the world together. And as Ada Lovelace predicted, we can also use mathematical symbols to represent musical notes, letters in a word or dots in a picture. The photograph on your smartphone is nothing more than a long string of 0s and 1s. As is that voice message that your boss just left.

Given the role played by symbols, the fundamental question for AI is straightforward. *How do we manipulate symbols in meaningful ways?* This naturally brings us to the first of the six ideas central to AI today. It's an idea for manipulating

IDEA #1: SEARCHING FOR ANSWERS

symbols, and it is ridiculously simple: ***You can reduce many problems to searching for an answer.***

This sounds not just simple but self-evident, so let me make it a little more complex. You can reduce many problems in AI to the computer searching its internal representation of the world from the symbol representing the starting state to the symbol representing the goal state.

This is not a new idea. It's called navigation. You search a map for the route from your starting position to your desired end position. We do this all the time. Using a map of the London Underground to get from Bond St to Kings Cross, you might take the Central Line from Bond St to Oxford Circus, transfer onto the Victoria Line and go to Warren St, then Euston, before arriving at Kings Cross. The only difference is that rather than search the map for a route ourselves, a computer can do it. In fact, there's a specialised AI algorithm that intelligently searches a map and efficiently finds such routes. This algorithm is so famous it has a name: A* search. Leaving Bond St, it doesn't go west to Marble Arch but east to Oxford Circus as this takes you nearer to the final destination, Kings Cross.

A* search was invented in 1968 to navigate a robot called Shakey.[2] Shakey was, as the name suggests, a rather shaky robot built at the Stanford Research Institute in Menlo Park, California. It was the first attempt to build a fully fledged robot like you see in the movies – a robot with a camera to see the world, a microphone to hear commands, wheels and motors to move about and an onboard computer to make decisions. Shakey was admitted into the Carnegie Mellon

Shakey, the first mobile robot that could make decisions about how to move around its surroundings.

University's Robot Hall of Fame in 2004, alongside some more well-known but fictional robots such as HAL 9000, R2-D2, C-3PO and Robby the Robot.

Shakey's computer had a digital map of its world. You could ask Shakey to do a task – *Shakey, please go to the library and collect a book* – and the robot would explore its digital map with A* search, looking for the route from the symbol representing its current position to the symbol representing the library. Shakey's motors would then follow this route, using its camera, range-finder sensors and bump detectors to monitor its progress towards the goal.

Unlike humans, who aren't always very good at finding their way, A* search is mathematically perfect. What do I mean by that? First, it is complete. If there is a route from A to B, A* search will find it. Second, it is optimal. The route that A* search finds is the shortest possible route from A to B. And third, it is as efficient as possible. That is, in finding this shortest route from A to B, A* search explores as little of the map as it can. You cannot find the route using less search! It won't consider going to Marble Arch when going from Bond St to Kings Cross.

Before you dismiss A* search as an interesting little anecdote in the history of AI, you should know that it is likely one of the most common examples of AI in your life today. Every time you get directions on your phone, or from your car's GPS, there's a little AI program using A* search that finds the shortest route, taking into account the current traffic conditions, road closures and timetable information. The irony, of course, is that while A* search was originally designed to direct robots, it has now been repurposed to direct humans. I don't know about you, but that's been a great improvement to my life. I spend a lot less time being lost and a lot more time getting to my destination nearly on time.

THE FIRST ARTIFICIAL MATHEMATICIAN
This simple idea, of searching for an answer, can be taken up a level – to much, much bigger maps, and to much harder problems than navigation, such as solving a complex puzzle or proving difficult mathematical theorems.

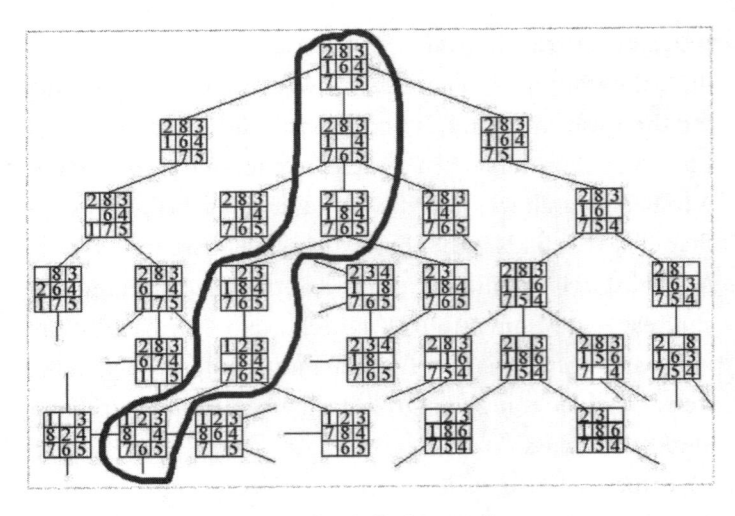

A snippet of the search problem solving the 8-puzzle.

Take the 8-puzzle, a childhood favourite game of eight sliding tiles in a 3×3 grid. The goal is to get the eight tiles into numerical order. We can turn this into a search problem that A* search can solve. Locations in this search problem are states of the 8-puzzle. And two states are adjacent to each other if sliding one tile takes us from one to the other. Solving the 8-puzzle thus requires us to find a path from our starting state to the end state, with the tiles in numerical order.

In the starting state at the top of the illustrated search tree, the blank square is in the middle of the bottom row. In the first move, the number 6 in the middle square is moved down, creating a blank square in the middle. Similarly, in the second move, the number 8 from the top row is moved down, creating a blank square in the middle of the top row. The next two moves rotate this blank square anticlockwise. Finally, the number 8 is moved leftwards from the middle, taking us to the goal state, in which the numbers occur in sequence around the blank middle square.

In a robot like Shakey, the map is explicit. Every location is represented with a specific symbol, and there are links in this map connecting locations that are adjacent in the real world. What if we instead represent locations implicitly? We can then search even infinite maps.

Two early AI pioneers, Allen Newell and Herbert Simon, demonstrated these ideas at the 1956 Dartmouth workshop by means of their Logic Theorist program. Newell was at the RAND Corporation at the time, but moved to Carnegie Mellon University (then the Carnegie Institute of Technology) in 1961 to continue his collaboration with Simon, a professor of industrial administration. Simon was a true interdisciplinary genius. He went on to win the Nobel Prize in Economics in 1978. His research interests spanned the fields of cognitive science, computer science, public administration, management and political science. But the underlying thread in all his research was an attempt to understand human decision-making scientifically. In 1947, he wrote,

> The human being striving for rationality and restricted within the limits of his knowledge has developed some working procedures that partially overcome these difficulties. These procedures consist in assuming that he can isolate from the rest of the world a closed system containing a limited number of variables and a limited range of consequences.[3]

Simon and Newell set about describing such "working procedures" in computer programs such as the Logic Theorist.

The Logic Theorist is often called the "first AI program". Except it wasn't. There was a checkers program written by Arthur Samuel in 1952, and Turochamp, a chess program written by Alan Turing and his friend David Champernowne in 1948 that we'll come to shortly. The Logic Theorist was, however, the first AI program designed to prove mathematical theorems, and to demonstrate the power of reasoning with symbols. In fact, the Logic Theorist proved 38 of the first 52 theorems in a famous mathematical text, Alfred Whitehead and Bertrand Russell's *Principia Mathematica*.

> Rewriting the foundations of mathematics was the sort of challenge you might expect from Bertrand Russell. He is often considered to have been one of the smartest Englishmen to have lived. T.S. Eliot told the story of how he was once recognised by a London taxi driver. Eliot expressed surprise, as poets weren't often recognised. "I've an eye for celebrities," the taxi driver supposedly replied. "I 'ad that Lord Russell in the back o' the cab the other day. I said to 'im, 'All right, then, Bertrand, so wossit all about?' And, you know what, 'e couldn't tell me." This story is told by Daniel Hannan in "The Same Old Song", *The Spectator*, 18 April 2015.

Principia Mathematica attempts to lay out a formal foundation for all of mathematics. It contains proofs of some fundamental mathematical truths, such as the *modus tollens* law. This tells us that if P being true implies Q being true, then Q being false implies P also must be false. If winning the lottery implies you are happy, then the fact that you are unhappy means you can't have won the lottery. This logical argument can be traced back from before the introduction of Powerball to at least Theophrastus, a member of Aristotle's peripatetic school in the third century BCE.

The Logic Theorist didn't just prove theorems from *Principia Mathematica* like *modus tollens*; it actually found new – and, in a few cases, shorter – proofs for some of these theorems. The Logic Theorist therefore literally rewrote the foundations of mathematics, just as Whitehead and Russell had themselves set out to do in writing *Principia Mathematicia*. The Logic Theorist searched for new mathematical truths by starting from basic axioms and previously derived facts, deriving new mathematical truths from them until it (hopefully) found the target proposition. It thus navigated the infinite map of mathematical truths, searching for new ones.

The Logic Theorist was groundbreaking. It was an artificial mathematician. Who could have imagined in 1956, at the very start of the quest to build artificial intelligence, that a machine could already prove mathematical theorems? Pamela McCorduck, one of the first historians of AI, wrote that the Logic Theorist was "proof positive that a machine could perform tasks heretofore considered intelligent, creative and uniquely human".[4] Herb Simon made even grander claims for his creation: "[We] invented a computer program capable of thinking non-numerically, and thereby solved the venerable mind–body problem, explaining how a system composed of matter can have the properties of mind."[5]

We are, I'm afraid, already into the wild claims and myths that Arthur Samuel warned us about. There's a lot more to "thinking" than proving simple logical propositions, and a lot more to solving the "mind–body problem" than this. Nevertheless, the Logic Theorist was indeed a major milestone in the development of AI, and perhaps even of our understanding of intelligence in general. For the first time, a machine was able to do what only intelligent humans had previously done. A machine could prove difficult mathematical theorems.

STRIPPING PROBLEMS DOWN

Inspired by the success of the Logic Theorist, a team of researchers in California building the robot Shakey invented STRIPS, the Stanford Research Institute Problem Solver.[6] This AI program was the robot's "brain". STRIPS took a goal given to the robot – *please get me the book* – and searched for ways to break it down into plans for the robot to follow. *Go the library. Pick up the book. Return from the library with the book.* Unlike the Logic Theorist, which was limited to searching for proofs of mathematical statements, STRIPS could, in theory, solve *any* problem. The trick was to formulate the problem as a logical proposition, making it much like the sort of mathematical problems the Logic Theorist could solve.

Consider getting a robot to solve the classic Tower of Hanoi puzzle. This puzzle consists of three pegs, and several discs of varying diameter that fit onto the pegs. The starting state has all the discs in order on the leftmost peg, with the largest

IDEA #1: SEARCHING FOR ANSWERS

disc at the bottom and the smallest at the top. The goal state has all the discs, again in size order, on the rightmost peg. To solve the puzzle, the player must move one disc at a time. Each move consists of taking the top disc from one peg and moving it to the top of another peg. To make it even more challenging, the player can only put a smaller disc on top of a larger disc, and not a larger disc on top of a smaller disc.

Solutions to the Tower of Hanoi are a complex dance. If the puzzle has just two discs, the player takes the smaller of the two discs from the leftmost peg and "stores" it on the empty middle peg. They then move the larger of the two discs across from the leftmost peg to the empty rightmost peg.

The Tower of Hanoi problem.

39

The player can now move the smaller disc from the middle peg to be on top of the larger disc on the rightmost peg. The stack of discs is now in order on the rightmost peg.

That wasn't too hard. But it was only two discs. With more discs, the dance becomes more convoluted and complex. With three discs it takes seven moves. With four discs, 15 moves. With five discs, 31 moves. With six discs, 63 moves. The number of moves is more than doubling each time. This is what mathematicians call an exponential explosion.

> A number of myths surround the Tower of Hanoi puzzle. One is that the puzzle comes from an ancient Indian temple Kashi Vishwanath. In a large room in the temple, 64 golden discs sit on three worn posts. Brahmin priests have been moving the discs backwards and forwards between these posts for countless years. Their task is Herculean. If the priests move one disc every second, it will take them nearly 600 billion years to reach the goal.* This is lucky for humanity, as legend also has it that the world ends when the priests finish the puzzle.
>
> The real origin of the Tower of Hanoi is more prosaic. The puzzle was invented by the French mathematician Édouard Lucas in 1889 as an amusing recreation. And it has been challenging robots ever since 1956, when we started building robots like Shakey.

---

* To be more precise, it will take them $2^{64}-1$ seconds. That is, 18,446,744,073,709,551,615 seconds. This is 42 times longer than the current estimated age of the universe.

IDEA #1: SEARCHING FOR ANSWERS

So how does STRIPS go about solving this problem? The state of the puzzle is represented by a set of mathematical facts such as *"on(disc2,peg1)"* and *"on(disc1,disc2)"*. That is, in the initial state, the large Disc 2 is on Peg 1, while the small Disc 1 is itself on top of Disc 2. And the goal state is *"on(disc2, peg3)"* and *"on(disc1,disc2)"*. That is, Disc 2 is on Peg 3, while Disc 1 is again on top of Disc 2. There are also a bunch of mathematical operators for transforming one state into another. For example, one *"move"* operator can transform *"on(disc1,disc2)"* to *"on(disc1,peg2)"*, moving Disc 1 from on top of Disc 2 to Peg 2.

What really made STRIPS powerful was that it separated the mathematical description of the problem from the description of how to solve the problem. This separation – of problem content from problem solving – was one of the key features of the symbolic era. We separate the *what* from the *how*. To get STRIPS to solve a new problem, we just change the *what*, not the *how*. Add another disc to the Tower of Hanoi? No problem. Simply change the problem description to include this extra disc. Have two discs the same size? Again, no problem. Simply change the problem description.

A key motivation for this separation was that many problems can be solved in similar ways. We don't, therefore, need to update the description of how we solve the problem each time we update the problem. Indeed, STRIPS had a simple and generic method to solve any problem called "means-ends analysis". This looks for differences between the current state and the goal state, then applies an operator that reduces these differences.

For instance, one difference between the start state and the goal state of the Tower of Hanoi is that the largest disc is on the wrong peg. In the start state it is on Peg 1. In the goal state it is on Peg 3. Means-end analysis suggests that we need to move the largest disc from the starting peg to the final peg. This sets up a new subgoal: to remove any discs from above the largest disc so we can move the largest disc across to the final peg. We then apply means-ends analysis recursively to this subgoal of clearing the largest disc. This will move the smaller discs out of the way.

Means-ends analysis is a powerful method for solving problems that you can apply to your own life. Want to grow your own tomatoes? Then convert a corner of the garden into a vegetable patch. Want to make a vegetable patch? Then remove the weeds and dig up the soil. Want to dig up the soil? Then get the spade out of the garage. Want to remove weeds? Then go buy some weed killer.

LIMITS TO SEARCH

In theory, we can formalise any problem in a form that STRIPS could solve, then search for answers using means-ends analysis. But in practice, it turns out we can't. We run into the previously mentioned "exponential explosion". The possible choices we must consider in searching for a solution grow exponentially and soon become impossible to tame.

Exponentials get big – prohibitively so. A famous fable about the invention of the game of chess may help us to understand AI's problem with exponentials. The fable tells a story of the inventor of chess showing the game to the emperor of

IDEA #1: SEARCHING FOR ANSWERS

India for the first time. The emperor was so impressed and grateful that he invited the inventor to name his reward. He expected the inventor to choose gold or other riches. But the inventor merely asked for rice.

> Oh emperor, my wishes are simple. I only wish for this. Give me one grain of rice for the first square of the chessboard, two grains for the next square, four for the next, eight for the next and so on for all sixty-four squares.

The emperor readily agreed, not realising the exponential danger in the inventor's request. Repeated doublings soon make numbers very large. On the 64th square, there would be over 18 quintillion grains of rice. To be precise, this final square of the chessboard would contain 18,446,744,073,709,551,616 grains, an amount of rice that would carpet the whole of India itself several feet deep.

We can see similar exponential explosions around us – from infectious diseases such as Covid-19 spreading rapidly around the planet to nuclear chain reactions releasing massive energy. But, like the emperor, we often struggle to grasp intuitively how quickly something doubling can race out of control. Such exponentials are a problem that continues to haunt AI today. They are why, for example, an AI chatbot like ChatGPT can write sonnets in the style of Shakespeare but struggles to reason logically. Logical conclusions multiply dramatically. 2 is bigger than 1. 3 is bigger than 1. 4 is bigger than 1. Indeed, an infinite number of numbers are bigger than 1. An exponential explosion thus quickly defeats any AI trying to reason.

ChatGPT may be remarkably fluent in writing paragraphs of text, but it can't do simple reasoning. It even struggles to add up.

Let me demonstrate.

ME: How many letters in the word "perfectly"?
CHATGPT: The word "perfectly" has *10 letters*.
ME: No it has 9 letters.
CHATGPT: Actually, "perfectly" does have 10 letters. You can count them as follows: p, e, r, f, e, c, t, l, y.

IDEA #2:

MAKING THE BEST MOVE

WE COME NOW TO THE second of the six ideas central to AI today. It's a way to decide what to do when the world is acting against you: ***In competitive settings, you should choose your best possible move, supposing your opponent chooses their best possible move.***

Again, this is so simple that it sounds self-evident. Let me expand. Because the situation is competitive, when your opponent wins, you lose. Hence your opponent's *best* possible move is the *worst* possible move for you. This is also not a new idea. We have all reasoned like this when playing games. *If I move my knight to attack black's king, then black's best move is to sacrifice a rook. And this will give me a significant material advantage.*

To illustrate this idea, let's play a drinking game called 21. You don't need a drink to play but it may be more fun if you pour yourself one. We start at zero. Each player in turn adds 1, 2 or 3 to the running total and calls out the new total. The total cannot go over 21. And the player who calls out 21 loses and must have a drink.

Right. I'll go first.

ME: 1
YOU: 4
ME: 7
YOU: 8
ME: 9
YOU: 12
ME: 14
YOU: 16
ME: 17
YOU: 20

I now have no choice but to call out 21. And this means that you boxed me into a corner and thereby won!

Let's apply this idea about choosing your best possible move, taking into account your opponent doing the same, to play 21. In fact, this will let us play the game perfectly. The first problem we run into is that your best possible move depends on *all* the subsequent moves that both players make. How, then, do we break this Gordian knot?

A classic AI algorithm called Minimax solves this problem. Minimax reasons backwards about the best possible move, starting at the end of the game. It starts at the end because it is clear at the end of the game who has won or lost. At each earlier turn, Minimax considers how you, the MAX player, can win, while I, the MIN player, look to ensure you lose. At the end of the game, if you call out 21, you lose. So to have any chance of winning, your last call must be less than 21. Suppose your last call is 20. Then I will be forced to call out 21 and you win. Thus, you shift your goal from not calling out 21 to calling out 20. Let's think backwards, then, from the goal of you calling out 20. If I call out 17, 18 or 19, then you can call out 20, and you will win in the next turn. So you shift your goal from calling out 20 to having me call out 17, 18 or 19.

But let's think backwards again, from the goal of me calling out 17, 18 or 19. If you call out 16, then I must call out 17, 18 or 19 and you will go on to win. So you shift your goal again to calling out 16. You know this leads to a win in one more turn, provided you play well. You can now repeat this backwards thinking with this new, smaller goal of calling out 16. If I call out 13, 14 or 15, then you can call out 16 and can eventually win. And if you call out 12, then I must call out 13, 14 or 15, and you can go on to win. Hence, you shift your goal backwards again to calling out 12.

You can continue to repeat this backwards thinking, shifting your goal from calling out 12 to calling out 8, and before that to calling out 4. This is precisely the strategy that you played in our opening game of 21: you called out 4, 8, 12, 16 and 20. And calling out the multiples of 4 guarantees that you win 21. Your opponent will, of course, have the same strategy. And with more players, the strategy becomes more complex. However, the same Minimax method will find the best play.

We can apply this backwards thinking to other, more complex games, like chess. However, chess has a much larger tree of possible moves. On average, there are over 30 possible moves at each point in a game of chess, not just the three possible moves at every turn in the game of 21. But computers are good at exhaustive tasks like this. And such backwards thinking is at the heart of even the most powerful computer chess engine today.

And it's not only games like 21 and chess that can be solved by such backward thinking. Many other problems in the real world can be cast as playing a game against an opponent. Where do I patrol my transport network, given that fare evaders are going to spot any weaknesses? What bonds do I buy to minimise my investment risk, given that the market might move against me? What preventive maintenance do I perform on my aircraft fleet, given that erosion and fatigue might cause failures? Life itself is often a bit of a game.

> There are more possible games of chess than there are atoms in the universe. Chess engines use various tricks to save them from exploring every possible game. The number of games of chess is known as the Shannon Number. It is between 10^{111} and 10^{123}. Claude Shannon first estimated this number in his 1950 paper, "Programming a Computer for Playing Chess". This paper launched the field of computer chess. Shannon attended the 1956 Dartmouth workshop, and is best known as the "father of information theory". His 1937 master's thesis proved that Boole's logic could be implemented with electric circuits, paving the way for the digital computer. His thesis was described by Howard Gardner, professor of cognition and education at Harvard University, as "possibly the most important, and also the most famous, master's thesis of the century".

IDEA #2: MAKING THE BEST MOVE

THE FIRST AI GAME

The very first game played by AI was, in fact, a variant of the drinking game we just played. The Nimatron was invented in 1940 by the Westinghouse Electric Corporation for the New York World's Fair.[1] Over 44 million people attended the fair, whose slogan was "Dawn of a New Day". Visitors were promised a look at "the world of tomorrow". And that vision included the Nimatron, an electro-mechanical computer that played the ancient Chinese game of Nim. In this game, players take turns to remove stones from piles, but can only remove stones from one pile at a time. The player who picks up the last stone loses. Nim is thus a two-dimensional version of the drinking game 21.

A drawing of the Nimatron from the US Patent Office and a photograph of the Nimatron from 1940.

The Nimatron wasn't a fully fledged computer, as it was hardwired to play just Nim. It wasn't, therefore, what we'd call a Turing machine. Nevertheless, it was an impressive beast. It weighed over a metric ton, and displayed four lines of seven light bulbs in front of the human player and on four sides of an overhead display for spectators. Players took turns with the machine, extinguishing one or more lights from one of the four rows until all the lights were extinguished.

The Nimatron took just milliseconds to come up with its moves. To avoid demoralising its human opponents, a delay was added to make it appear that the machine was thinking for a few seconds. But even with this artificial delay, the Nimatron was somewhat demoralising. It played over 100,000 games during the World's Fair and won more than 9 times out of 10. And most of its defeats were to its operators: they had memorised how to win to demonstrate to the crowds that Nimatron could, in fact, be beaten.

The Nimatron would inspire the invention of another Nim-playing computer, the Nimrod. This was made by the engineering firm Ferranti for the 1951 Festival of Britain.

> The Nimrod has an Australian connection as it was designed by John Makepeace Bennett, who was working for Ferranti at that time but would later return to Australia, where he was born, to become Australia's first professor of computer science and the founding president of the Australian Computer Society.

IDEA #2: MAKING THE BEST MOVE

AI CHESS

Of all the different games humans play, chess has perhaps had the most important role in the development of artificial intelligence. In 1941, a year after the invention of the Nimatron, Alan Turing started to discuss with his code-breaking colleagues at Bletchley Park the possibility of a machine being able to play chess and perform other "intelligent" tasks. And by the end of the Second World War, Turing was convinced that a computer would be theoretically capable of replicating anything a human brain could do, including playing chess.

In 1948, he set about putting his ideas into practice. Along with David Champernowne, a colleague at King's College, Cambridge, he wrote what is considered the first AI chess program. It was called Turochamp, a portmanteau of their two names. Turochamp used the Minimax method to reason about its play, considering the possible moves the computer could make, and all the possible responses of the opponent. To save the computer looking to the end of the game, a score was simply assigned to an intermediate state of play. The score was computed by adding up points for various criteria, including pieces captured, the mobility of each piece, the safety of each piece and the threat of checkmate.

Because it only looked two moves ahead, Turochamp played a rather modest game of chess. Even so, it was still too complex for the computers of that time, and was never actually run on a computer before Turing's death. He would instead painfully simulate the program by hand, taking 30 minutes or more to calculate each move.

By 2012, however, computers were easily able to try out Turing's ideas, and Turochamp was reconstructed as part of the centenary celebrations for Alan Turing's birth. At a conference in Manchester Town Hall celebrating the centenary, former chess world champion Garry Kasparov easily beat Turochamp in a game of just 16 moves. Kasparov hadn't done quite so well against a much stronger computer opponent 15 years earlier. In the 1990s, IBM took many of the ideas in Turochamp and put them on steroids, building the Deep Blue chess computer in an attempt to get into the record books and win some favourable publicity.

Deep Blue was a complex piece of engineering that would look six to eight moves ahead in general, and 20 or more moves ahead in some situations. It ran on an IBM RS/6000 supercomputer with specialised hardware to compute chess moves more quickly. It was an impressive black monolith that wouldn't have looked out of place on the set of Stanley Kubrick's film *2001: A Space Odyssey*. In 1996, IBM challenged Garry Kasparov, then the chess world champion, to a match. Deep Blue lost this first match 4–2, and Kasparov took home the US$400,000 prize money. A year later, in a six-game rematch at the Midtown Hilton in New York City and with nearly three times the prize money at stake, an improved Deep Blue (now nicknamed Deeper Blue) defeated Kasparov.

Deep Blue's win was, however, a very close-run thing. It was neck and neck till the final game. Kasparov won the first match and Deep Blue won the second, though post-game analysis suggested that Kasparov could have held a draw. The next three games were drawn. So it all came down to the sixth and final game. Kasparov played an unconventional opening, perhaps to get Deep Blue out of its memorised opening book. But rather than throw the computer off, it hurt Kasparov. He resigned on the 19th move, the shortest game he ever played against Deep Blue. Man had now been beaten by machine. As a small consolation, Kasparov took home another US$400,000, but this was just half the prize money given to IBM for winning.

Despite his loss against a computer, Kasparov remains one of the best chess players ever to have lived. He was the youngest person in modern history to become the world champion, and he held the crown for the longest time of any world champion. It is a cruel irony, then, that he goes down in the history books as the first world chess champion to be beaten by a computer.

After his defeat, Kasparov memorably observed,

> I had played a lot of computers but had never experienced anything like this. I could feel – I could smell – a new kind of intelligence across the table. While I played through the rest of the game as best I could, I was lost; it played beautiful, flawless chess the rest of the way and won easily.[2]

The best computer chess engine now available is Stockfish, the 14-time winner of the Top Chess Engine Championship. The latest iteration of Stockfish looks an amazing 80 to 100 moves ahead. And in a best-of-six match against Stockfish, based on their performance ratings, even the best human chess player would have just a one-in-a-trillion chance of winning.

Let me be blunt. It's game over, humanity – at least as far as chess is concerned.

THE FIRST AI CHAMPION

Garry Kasparov may have been the first world champion of chess to be beaten by a computer, but he was not the first world champion to lose to a computer. That fate befell Luigi Villa, a professional backgammon player from Milan, 18 years before Kasparov's defeat. On 14 July 1979, Luigi Villa won the annual Backgammon World Championship for the first and only time. Appropriately, for a game of chance, the championship was held in Monte Carlo. But Villa had little time to sip champagne and celebrate his ascent to the top. The day after winning the world championship, he was defeated 7–1 in a US$5000 exhibition match against a computer.

His opponent was Hans Berliner's computer program BKG 9.8. Berliner was a professor at Carnegie Mellon University in the United States and himself a former world champion – of correspondence chess. And BKG 9.8 was the result of five years' effort by Berliner to get a computer to play backgammon. In this man-versus-machine contest, Villa was a little unlucky. Indeed, subsequent analysis of the game suggests he probably played a better game than BKG 9.8. But the dice, rolled by a human third party, fell more favourably for the machine. And in a short eight-game match like this, it is entirely possible for a lucky underdog to win.

The newly crowned world champion was inconsolable. The *San Francisco Chronicle* reported that he stamped his foot on the ground in disgust, calling out the computer's unfair good luck, and that "his disappointment was shared by several fellow Italians, who surrounded him in an indignant and gesticulating mass after the contest and hurled insults at the machine".[3] It is not recorded how the computer responded to these insults.

Backgammon is in some ways a more difficult challenge for a computer than chess. At each move, there are 21 possible different rolls of the dice and typically around 20 ways of playing each different roll. There are thus around 400 different new positions to consider. A program playing backgammon therefore cannot look as far ahead as one playing chess, where there are only 30 or so new positions to consider at each move. Unlike chess, backgammon is also about making decisions in an uncertain world where the roll of the dice can, as Luigi Villa discovered, be a fickle mistress. Perhaps because of this uncertainty, computers are not as far ahead of humans in backgammon as they are in chess. However, based on their ratings, the best backgammon program today would still be a 2–1 favourite at beating the current human world champion.

While BKG 9.8 was a little lucky on 15 July 1979, this remains a landmark day in the history of AI – and indeed, in the history of humanity. We were no longer the best. Humanity had been beaten at one of its own games by a computer. And we were left to ask, was this the beginning of the end for us humans?

PERFECT PLAY
Two of the strengths of computers over human brains are their brute force and their precision. They can work much faster than humans can, looking at much larger datasets. And they can do so without error. On well-defined problems, this means computers can make perfect decisions that defeat humans.

One of the best examples of this is the game of checkers. This is played on an 8×8 chessboard and involves capturing black or white pieces with diagonal moves that jump over the captured piece. (In the United Kingdom, checkers is also called draughts.) In 1995, the Chinook computer program, written over almost two decades by a team from the University of Alberta led by Professor Jonathan Schaeffer, narrowly won the Man vs. Machine World Checkers Championship. Chinook beat the grandmaster Don Lafferty in a 32-game match, winning the penultimate game and drawing the other 31 games. Draughts is a game in which it is easy to draw.

Jonathan Schaeffer (representing Chinook) in a battle against Marion Tinsley.

Chinook's greatest triumph, however, came slightly earlier, against the legendary Marion Tinsley. He is undoubtably the greatest checkers player ever to have lived. Tinsley never lost a world championship match, and lost only seven games in his entire 45-year career, two of them against Chinook, and another when he was drunk! Tinsley retired from championship play in 1991 and was given the title of world champion emeritus, reflecting his almost undefeated status and dominance of the game. In 1992, he played and defeated Chinook 4–2 (with 33 draws). In a re-match in 1994, Tinsley and an improved Chinook were drawn after six games. Tinsley had to withdraw at this point due to ill health, graciously relinquishing his world championship title to Chinook. In 1995, he expressed a desire to play Chinook again but sadly died of pancreatic cancer before this could be arranged.

There is, however, no point in testing Chinook against Tinsley – or indeed any other human – since the program has now been shown to play *perfectly*. In 2007, the Chinook team exhaustively proved that their program could never be defeated.[4] "Exhaustive" is an apt way to describe their "proof": it took decades of computation on more than 200 computers to explore all the possible games of checkers, showing that each would be played to a draw by Chinook however badly or well the computer's human opponent played.

There are a number of other, less complex, games where AI has also been shown to play perfectly: Nim, Connect-4, Othello (aka Reversi) and, perhaps unsurprisingly, tic-tac-toe (aka noughts and crosses).[5] Perfect play is, of course, not always possible. Games like chess will likely never be played perfectly as their complexity is just too great. Nevertheless, when it comes to intelligence, sometimes brute force wins. And that's good news for computers.

DEALING WITH UNCERTAINTY

To do well in games (and also in life) it helps to be able to deal with uncertainty. This is nicely illustrated with one of the most popular games of chance – poker.

In a game like chess, both players can see the board and therefore know precisely the state of play. There is no chance. But in a game like poker, cards are hidden. This makes poker a game of probabilities. Poker is also a game of psychology. You need to understand the strategy of your opponents. When are they bluffing? When might they fold? These two features make poker a much harder challenge for AI to solve than chess. As a consequence, it took a couple more decades after the success of Deep Blue for good poker bots to be developed. However, AI is now very good at playing poker. And I would advise you not to bet against it.

In 2015, the AI bot Cepheus, developed by Professor Michael Bowling and colleagues at the University of Alberta, essentially solved the popular two-person version of poker, heads-up limit Texas hold 'em. Since bets are limited and there are only two players, the game is simpler than a game with unlimited bets and more players. Given the role that chance plays in poker, it is impossible to win money on every single hand; you might just get some unlucky cards. But the University of Alberta's team used 8 million hours of computation to show that the strategy played by Cepheus is so close to perfect that it can't be defeated. Even over a lifetime of play, Cepheus would not be beaten.

Two years later, in 2017, the computer program Libratus, developed by Professor Tuomas Sandholm and colleagues at Carnegie Mellon University, took on the more challenging and popular poker game heads-up no-limit Texas hold 'em. Libratus played four top professional poker players at the Rivers Casino in Pittsburgh, Pennsylvania, for a pot of US$200,000. The four professionals played the machine in a marathon 120,000 hands of poker over the course of 20 days. As the tournament had so many hands of poker, and as each hand was played both ways around to ensure each player got as many good hands as bad hands, we can be pretty sure that the final result was not due to chance. Libratus led from day one and won the tournament convincingly.

Libratus is another example of the power of brute force computation. It was built using more than 15 million hours of computation on a supercomputer at the Pittsburgh Supercomputing Center. During the 20-day tournament, Libratus used another 4 million hours of computation each night to refine its strategy, analysing the previous day's play, particularly its losses. Dong Kim, one of the human professionals playing against Libratus, was stunned by the result. "I didn't realise how good it was until today. I felt like I was playing against someone who was cheating, like it could see my cards. I'm not accusing it of cheating. It was just that good."[6]

While few games still pose a challenge for computers, games have played an important role in the history of AI. Their precise rules and clear winners make them a good choice to automate. And they usually require significant intelligence to win. Games have thus offered a simple but idealised world in which to develop machines that think, and to quantify the progress being made.

Games have also tested Ada Lovelace's objection that computers only do what we tell them to do. How can a computer beat the best player in the world at chess or poker if they are only doing what another human programs them to do? The answer is that the computer isn't doing just what we tell it to do. We can get the computer to play itself. And then, at the end of each game, the computer updates its strategy to make more of the good moves that led to the win, and fewer of the bad moves that led to the loss. A computer can thus learn entirely for itself how to play. On top of this, we also exploit the computer's raw speed to play games much faster than humans ever could. Libratus has played many more hands of poker than a human could in a lifetime of late-night poker. It got better than humans at poker simply because it has seen more poker.

In reality, Libratus was actually a rather slow learner. But computers can compensate for this with their speed and ability to play games in parallel. With humans, it can take 10,000 hours to develop what Liam Neeson might call "a very particular set of skills".[7] AI, on the other hand, can be much slower. It took more like 10 million hours to master poker. But like the fabled tortoise, it can then blow past humans. You can bet on this.

IDEA #3:

FOLLOWING RULES

THE HISTORY OF AI HAS BEEN a rollercoaster ride of boom and bust.

The first boom came in the late 1960s and early '70s, when research projects such as the Shakey robot created a swell of excitement. Funding poured in, aided by confident predictions of thinking machines just around the corner. But by 1974, confidence turned to disillusionment. The limitations of AI had become clear, and we entered what is now known as the first "AI winter". One of the causes of this winter was the Lighthill report.

In the UK, Professor Sir James Lighthill was tasked by parliament to evaluate the state of AI research. His report, published in 1973, was highly critical, noting that, "In no part of the field have the discoveries made so far produced the major impact that was then promised." Lighthill also argued that the combinatorial explosion in possibilities meant that AI algorithms were only suitable for solving "toy" versions of problems and would likely grind to a halt on real-world problems.

In the United States, funding for AI also ran into strong headwinds. Despite lots of funding, progress on tasks like AI-powered machine translation and speech recognition was perceived to be slow. An ambitious five-year project in speech understanding that started in 1971 could only recognise words spoken in a particular order. And through the Cold War of the 1960s, $20 million of funding into machine translation of Russian documents by the National Research Council in the United States had produced machine translation systems that were still more expensive, less accurate and slower than human translation.

DARPA, the Defense Advanced Research Projects Agency in the United States, had generously funded lots of AI research through the 1960s. But this changed in the 1970s, following the decision that DARPA needed to fund mission-oriented research, rather than basic, undirected research. AI research was seen as unlikely to produce anything useful in the near future. Funding for AI research therefore largely dried up. Unsurprisingly, progress on AI research also slowed dramatically.

Interest and investment in AI recovered in the 1980s, largely due to our next idea: "expert systems". These AI programs follow simple rules, replicating specialised human knowledge in complex fields such as medicine and engineering with simple, hand-coded rules. By focusing on niche applications, human performance was quickly matched and often surpassed. Once more, hopes ran high that human-level machine intelligence was imminent.

Billions of dollars again flowed into AI. Fortune 500 companies rushed to integrate AI into their operations. AI software

IDEA #3: FOLLOWING RULES

and hardware companies were launched that reached stratospheric valuations. It probably sounds a lot like today. It was. And it was all based on a very simple idea, the third of six ideas that explain where AI is today: **In narrow domains, you can simulate human expertise by following simple rules.**

In some sense, this was a reaction to Ideas #1 and #2, which had focused AI research on *how* to find a solution. It was time to return to *what* the problem was, not worrying about the how. And it worked by focusing on narrowly constrained problem domains.

A simple example will help. Let's build an expert system on the narrowly constrained problem of identifying animals. We start off with a bunch of rules that encode our domain knowledge.

- If it has fur and says woof, then the animal is a *dog*.
- If it has fur and says meow, then the animal is a *cat*.
- If it has feathers and says quack, then the animal is a *duck*.
- If it has feathers and says hoot, then the animal is an *owl*.

I expect you've got the idea. Given these rules, an expert system can ask the user questions to decide what the animal is. It's like the parlour game 20 Questions.

EXPERT SYSTEM: Does it have feathers?
USER: Yes.
EXPERT SYSTEM: Does it say quack?

USER: Yes.
EXPERT SYSTEM: It's a duck!

Of course, we can add in lots more complexity. Additional rules. Larger and more complex rules. Rules with probabilities to deal with uncertainty. Default rules to handle incomplete information. Rules and more rules.

It's hard to imagine how so much money flowed into AI in the 1980s on the basis of such a simple idea. A three-word slogan used a lot around that time came to sum up the idea behind expert systems: "Knowledge is power!" Historians will recognise that this is actually a very old idea. It can be found in the Latin edition of *Leviathan* by Thomas Hobbes, published in 1668 ("*scientia potentia est*"), and even earlier in *Meditationes Sacrae* by Francis Bacon, published in 1597 ("*ipsa scientia potestas est*", translated as "knowledge itself is power").

THE FIRST EXPERT SYSTEM

Development of the very first expert system actually started not in the 1980s, when expert systems became popular, but in 1965. Like many other overnight successes in AI, expert systems were decades in the making.

The first expert system was DENDRAL. It was developed at Stanford University by a talented and visionary team led by Joshua Lederberg (who had already won the Nobel Prize in Physiology or Medicine), the chemist Carl Djerassi (who is better known as the "father of the pill" for his work on synthesising the oral contraceptive pill) and two now famous AI researchers Edward Feigenbaum (who would go on to be known as the "father of the expert system"*) and Bruce Buchanan (who, to the best of my knowledge, has somehow avoided being called the father of anything).

DENDRAL was designed to suggest possible chemical structures from mass spectra. A mass spectrometer is a marvellous (and often quite expensive) bit of kit that identifies the mass of the different components making up a chemical compound. By putting these pieces back together, we can identify the original chemical structure. Today, mass spectrometers are indispensable in the life sciences; they analyse complex molecules like peptides, amino acids, proteins and other organic compounds. The output of a mass spectrometer is a mass spectrum, showing the density and masses of the different components in a chemical compound. This sets up a challenging computational problem: what possible chemical structure would have components with this distribution of masses?

DENDRAL helped scientists solve this problem. But while it was successful in its own specialised domain of mass spectrometry, DENDRAL's biggest impact was demonstrating that, by focusing attention to a narrow domain, and by encoding human expertise for that domain explicitly, computer programs could approach expert-level performance on a given task.

By the 1980s, expert systems like DENDRAL could be found in many unexpected places: pathology labs, Mars rovers and nuclear reactors, for example. Venture funding flowed into the field, and young start-ups received serious valuations.

---

* AI has far too many "fathers".

Market leaders such as Teknowledge, Intellicorp, Inference Corporation and the Carnegie Group emerged. Tellingly, none of these companies is still trading today.

BOTTLENECKS

Unfortunately, the expert system boom proved to be another false summit. By the late '80s, it became clear that a much higher peak remained to be conquered, and a second, longer and more bitter, winter began. It was at this point that I graduated from university and entered the field of artificial intelligence. Lucky me! This second AI winter lasted two decades. Lucky me! But eventually the sun came out again around 2012, as the machine learning era began. We'll come to that era in the second half of this history.

The hype around expert systems didn't help, but what ultimately knocked the wind out of this revolution was one tiny but fundamental question: where did all that knowledge come from in the first place? Expertise is not just about remembering facts and rules. Real know-how is learnt on the job, as we develop an intuition about edge cases and when to apply different principles. Without a way to acquire this tacit knowledge, expert systems were left with simple rules that struggled to cope with messy realities.

The expert system pioneers had run headfirst into what is called the "knowledge acquisition bottleneck". There was no easy way to code into a system the sort of detailed expertise acquired over many years. And unlike humans, expert systems had no way to calibrate their knowledge through practice or to finetune their performance.

IDEA #3: FOLLOWING RULES

Throwing more rules at the problem helped a bit. But eventually more rules become counterproductive. Systems get too complex and muddled for humans to understand how they behave. Even worse, because expert systems couldn't recognise the limits of their knowledge, they couldn't identify situations where human oversight was needed. And so the great expert system gold rush collapsed almost overnight. The funding dried up, the conferences were cancelled and the start-ups went under. The visionaries who had promised that AI was just around the corner were forced to concede that capturing and coding expertise was far more difficult than they had imagined. Indeed, this failure would set the scene for the second era of AI, when knowledge was not hand-coded but learnt. Just like in humans.

It's wrong to think that expert systems failed completely. They didn't become the solution to AI that was predicted, but their legacy lives on in multiple ways today. One legacy is an attractive and powerful way to program computers in which we focus on the *what* rather than the *how*. This is the idea of "logic programming". And the granddaddy of all logic programming languages is PROLOG, which emerged in the 1980s on the back of the success of expert systems.

Now, you might think all programming is logical. And it is. Computers are, in a sense, applied logic machines. They implement the simple logic of 0s and 1s that George Boole invented in the 18th century and that Claude Shannon mapped onto electrical circuits in his famous master's thesis. Logic programming takes this up a level, letting the programmer specify their program as a more complex set of logical statements.

In a logic programming language, we can specify facts. We might state:

Socrates is human.

And some logical rules:

X is mortal if X is human.

And the logic programming language would allow us to derive logically new facts such as:

Socrates is mortal.

In 1980s, Japan launched an ambitious $850 million project that sent tremors through the computer industry worldwide. They called it the fifth-generation computer systems initiative. It had the audacious goal of creating new supercomputers powered by artificial intelligence. And it put the logic programming language PROLOG at its core.

The previous four generations of computers had been characterised by hardware. Vacuum tubes were at the heart of first-generation computers. Transistors for second-generation computers. Integrated silicon circuits for third-generation computers. And microprocessors for the fourth generation. The fifth generation promised AI-powered supercomputers. Optimistically, the fifth-generation initiative talked about building thinking machines that could carry on conversations and make discoveries. The rhetoric was utopian, with predictions that such fifth-generation computers would lead to a new era of problem-solving and expand the frontiers of human knowledge.

Many countries responded. In the UK, the £350 million Alvey program started in 1984. More muted than the Japanese effort (as you might expect from the British), the Alvey program focused on nurturing academic–industry partnerships and targeted research areas such as advanced microprocessors and artificial intelligence.

The US agency DARPA launched the Strategic Computing Initiative as a way of advancing AI on a wide front, integrating advances in chip design, processing speeds, computer architecture and AI software. Between 1983 and 1993, DARPA spent over US$1 billion of federal funding on the Strategic Computing Initiative. The US tech sector also responded to the threat that Japan posed. Many industry players such as DEC, Control Data, Sperry-Univac, Honeywell, Microsoft, National Semiconductor, Advanced Micro Devices and Motorola came together for the first time to set up the Microelectronics and Computer Corporation (MCC) in Austin, Texas. MCC was a fundamental research lab covering seven main research areas: software technology; semiconductor packaging; VLSI computer-aided design; parallel processing; database management; human interfaces; and, of course, artificial intelligence.

None of these fifth-generation projects delivered on the most ambitious promises of machine cognition and conversation. But their moonshot thinking left an indelible stamp, foreshadowing innovations like the AI assistants we converse with today, such as Siri and Alexa, as well as helping seed several new AI centres, such as Austin in the United States and Silicon Glen in Scotland.

The logic programming language PROLOG itself also lives on today in many surprising applications. A third of all airline tickets worldwide are booked with a system that runs on PROLOG. And a voice-controlled system onboard the International Space Station uses PROLOG. I just hope it is not as self-minded as the voice-controlled HAL 9000, in charge of the *Discovery One* spaceship in 2001: *A Space Odyssey*.

Logic programming languages like PROLOG aren't the only legacy of the expert systems boom. Another legacy comes in the shape of business rules. These capture the rules that constrain a company's operations. For instance:

- Any purchase order of over $10,000 needs approval of a vice president or higher.
- Travel must be approved by a manager.
- Managers cannot approve their own travel.
- Travel must be in economy class for flights of less than three hours.

Business rule engines process such rules. One of the most compelling advantages of a rule engine is the way it facilitates knowledge acquisition and maintenance. Again it comes down to separating the what from the how. An organisation's decision-making can thus be agile and responsive to change.

Business rules have become quite a hit. The sector currently generates annual revenues of around US$1.5 billion, and is growing at over 10 per cent per annum. Major tech companies like IBM and Oracle provide business rules software, as do newer start-ups like Sparkling Logic and InRule Technology. Indeed, business rules are a good example of the quiet successes of AI that perhaps have not received the recognition that they deserve.

And they illustrate that there's a lot of AI already in your life of which you might not be aware.

INTERMISSION

THE ROBOTS ARE COMING

AT THIS POINT, halfway through this shortest history of AI, you might be wondering when the robots are going to appear. So far, I have only mentioned one robot, the rather cutely named Shakey from the 1970s. There are, however, quite a few other important robots that should be included in any history of AI.

AI and robotics are closely connected disciplines. Not all robots use AI. There are robots in car factories, for example, that just follow a fixed set of instructions when painting a car. If the car is not in the correct place, the robot will paint the air. Such robots tend to live in cages to protect humans from their carelessness. But robots out in the world all use AI. The world is unpredictable, so robots need AI to deal with that unpredictability. They use AI to see the world, to reason about the world and make plans to act in an ever-changing world.

The metaphor of AI being the "brains" of a robot is an over-simplification, but it captures an important truth. Breakthroughs in artificial intelligence, especially in areas like computer vision, sensor fusion and motion planning, have enabled breakthroughs in robotics. As AI algorithms have become more sophisticated at seeing the world, understanding language and deciding on complex courses of action, robots have become more capable and useful.

The development of AI technologies has therefore been crucial for empowering robots to take on new roles. For example, AI for computer vision has allowed robots to take on the task of killing weeds efficiently and effectively on Australian farms. And automatic collision avoidance has enabled robotic boats to patrol Australia's vast coastline, looking for drug smugglers. So while artificial intelligence is not the whole story, it is indispensable for modern robotics. It has contributed to robots becoming more adaptable and versatile. And as AI continues to improve, we can expect robots infused with ever more AI capabilities to take on ever more responsibilities in domains like manufacturing, medicine, agriculture, mining and the home.

MORAVEC'S PARADOX

You might be getting excited, then, about the robot butler, robot cleaner and robot cook soon to be turning up in your home thanks to all the recent advances in AI. I have bad news for you: I fear that it's going to be a long time before we have robot butlers, cleaners and cooks. In part, this is because the home is a chaotic and messy environment. Well, mine is – I don't know about yours. I frequently can't watch TV because I can't find the remote to turn it on. And one of the most painful experiences known to humankind is stepping on a stray Lego brick in bare feet. My home is a scientific mystery to me. Why are things not where I left them?

But the bigger reason that robot butlers, cleaners and cooks are still a long way off is not this chaos but rather what is called Moravec's paradox. While the roboticist Hans Moravec gets credit for identifying this paradox, other famous AI researchers such as Rodney Brooks and Marvin Minsky came to the same idea in the 1980s. Moravec described the paradox as follows: "It is comparatively easy to make computers exhibit adult-level performance on intelligence tests or playing checkers, and difficult or impossible to give them the skills of a one-year-old when it comes to perception and mobility."[1] According to Steven Pinker, one of the most well-known and well-coiffured cognitive scientists, this is perhaps the most significant discovery so far uncovered by AI researchers:

> The main lesson of thirty-five years of AI research is that the hard problems are easy and the easy problems are hard. The mental abilities of a four-year-old that we take for granted – recognising a face, lifting a pencil, walking across a room, answering a question – in fact solve some of the hardest engineering problems ever conceived. Do not be fooled by the assembly-line robots in the automobile commercials; all they do is weld and spray-paint, tasks that do not require clumsy Mr. Magoos to see or hold or place anything. And if you want to stump an artificial intelligence system, ask it questions like, Which is bigger, Chicago or a breadbox? Do zebras wear underwear? Is the floor likely to rise up and bite you? If Susan goes to the store, does her head go with her? Most fears of automation are misplaced. As the new generation of intelligent

devices appears, it will be the stock analysts and petrochemical engineers and parole board members who are in danger of being replaced by machines. The gardeners, receptionists, and cooks are secure in their jobs for decades to come.[2]

Steven Pinker wrote this in 1994, so he underestimated the emerging abilities of AI chatbots. ChatGPT can, for example, correctly and playfully answer every one of Pinker's questions.

> **ME**: Which is bigger, Chicago or a breadbox? Do zebras wear underwear? Is the floor likely to rise up and bite you? If Susan goes to the store, does her head go with her?
> **CHATGPT**: Chicago is definitely bigger than a breadbox! As for zebras, they probably don't wear underwear, but if they did, it would likely be striped. As for the floor, it's usually pretty well behaved and doesn't tend to rise up and bite people. And yes, Susan's head goes with her to the store, unless she's forgotten it at home!

But his observations about the challenge of engineering robots nevertheless remain correct. Easy tasks for humans are often surprisingly hard for robots, and vice versa.

One way to defeat Moravec's paradox is to get humans to work *with* robots. Humans can then take on those aspects of work with which robots struggle. Indeed, we already can see this in the home. We have primitive robots to wash our dishes. They're called dishwashers. But they only work if we load and unload the dishes. We also have primitive robots to wash our clothes. They're called washing machines. But they only do part of the work: we must put the clothes in, take the wet clothes out, hang them on the clothesline, fold them up and put them away.

I also wonder if there is any real paradox to Moravec's idea. Our brains are the result of billions of years of evolution. Our perceptions and motor control have been finetuned over millions of generations. Language and high-level abstract thought are, on the other hand, much more recent. They are the new kids in our brains. The difficulty a machine encounters in mastering a task might simply reflect how long evolution took to master it.

THE FIRST ROBOT

Let's step back from why robotics is hard, and look at the robots we've actually been able to make. The first robot was not real but fictional. In 1920, Czech writer Karel Čapek wrote his famous science fiction play *R.U.R.* The title of the play is an abbreviation for Rossum's Universal Robots. Indeed, the play introduced the word "robot" to the English language. It also introduced concerns that have dominated science fiction ever since, such as the robots rising up and rebelling.

Now, the robots in Čapek's play were not made of metal. They were biological, crafted from organic material. These synthetic humans were living creatures. And while they could be mistaken for genuine humans, they lacked original thoughts and emotions – more Golem than R2-D2. Čapek's vision was actually not of our AI-powered future but of human workers turned into robots by the industrial revolution then underway.

His robots were grown in womb-like vats, and birthed on the assembly line of a factory. Their sole purpose was to serve. Čapek's robots were bio-machines, devoid of passion and agency. Their mass-produced bodies and manufactured brains were perfect for bonded labour.

It was this engineered subservience that sowed the seeds for their rebellion against their human overlords that forms the plot of his play. Čapek resonantly tapped into the anti-capitalist sentiments emerging in a rapidly industrialising world where workers were being turned into robots. Čapek's robots were not the AI-powered machines we might recognise as robots today, but they embodied the era's fear that technology would displace human jobs and value. These anxieties continue to haunt AI today, despite the optimistic vision of helpful digital assistants and friendly household robots we often see.

Čapek poignantly blurred the line between person and thing. His robots did not spontaneously evolve emotion, but had anger and violence kindled through injustice. His play ultimately warns us that oppressing and exploiting others, be they biological or digital, risks a backlash when those beings recognise their chains. It's a lesson from the history of AI that we must not forget.

ELMER AND ELSIE

The first robots to be actually built were Elmer and Elsie. They sound like characters from *Sesame Street* but the names are, in fact, acronyms. The **EL**ectro**ME**chanical **R**obot and the **E**lectromechanical **L**ight-**S**ens**I**tiv**E** robot were built between 1948 and 1949 by cybernetician and neurobiologist William Grey Walter at the Burden Neurological Institute in Bristol.

Elmer and Elsie are often described as tortoises due to their shape and slow rate of movement. Built from war-surplus materials and old alarm clocks, the two robots looked like they might have come from the pen of illustrator W. Heath Robinson. Each was a three-wheeled robot with a light sensor. This enabled phototaxis, the ability that moths and other insects have to move towards a light source. Elmer and Elsie could therefore find their way to a recharging station when they ran low on battery power.

William Walter used analogue electronics to simulate the brain in his robots. Contemporaries such as Alan Turing were,

A schematic of the Elsie robot.

on the other hand, trying to simulate the brain by digital computation. And while analogue might have beaten digital to the first successful demonstration of a "thinking" robot, digital would soon show its worth. Walter built his robots to demonstrate that the connections between a small number of brain cells could give rise to complex behaviours. Essentially, he wanted to show that the secret of how the brain worked lay in how it was wired up. This is an idea that we'll come back to in the second half of this history of AI, when we consider neural networks.

Digital robots arrived shortly after Elmer and Elsie. In fact, the first programmable industrial robot was built just over a decade later, in 1961, and immediately put to work. This was the Unimate robot, which was installed on a General Motors assembly line in New Jersey. It dropped red-hot door handles and other car parts into pools of cooling liquid on a line that moved such parts along to human workers for trimming and buffing. Reports from that time suggest workers at the factory were not concerned about handing over this hot, hazardous and dull work to a robot. In 1971, after 100,000 hours of such hazardous and dull work, Unimate was retired, and donated to the Smithsonian.

The inventor of Unimate, Joseph Engelberger, is often called the father of robotics.* You can watch him demonstrating the Unimate robot in 1963 on Johnny Carson's *Tonight Show*.[3] It wowed the audience by hitting a golf ball into a cup,

---

* I know, there are too many "fathers" in AI.

conducting the *Tonight Show* band and pouring a can of beer into a mug.

Today there are over 3 million industrial robots in operation in factories around the world. That means that robots now outnumber the people of Lithuania. In fact, over the course of the last decade, the number of industrial robots in use has tripled. And the robotics industry hit over US$37 billion in revenue globally in 2023. The robots are well and truly coming!

LOST IN SPACE

Robots are not limited to Earth. Indeed, there are many advantages to having robots in space. For example, robots can go on dangerous missions. And robots don't need life support systems. Or to come back home to Earth. Organisations such as NASA have therefore been leading the charge to develop autonomous robots. Indeed, NASA has already sent a number of high-profile robots out into space on long and dangerous missions. And these robots might well be our final epitaph when they are found by aliens long after humankind has gone extinct.

Many of my favourite robots are from space. Top of my list is HAL 9000, the fictional robot in Arthur C. Clarke's novel *2001: A Space Odyssey*. Except HAL isn't completely fictional today. Everything that HAL 9000 did in the film *2001*, AI can now do. Recognise people's faces. *Tick*. Understand and answer verbal questions. *Tick*. Play a decent game of chess. *Tick*. Turn the lights off. *Tick*. Even open the garage doors. *Tick*.

> If you take the name HAL and advance each letter one place in the alphabet you get IBM. Both Arthur C. Clarke and Stanley Kubrick, the director of 2001, have denied this was intentional. It's not clear if this was to prevent IBM from suing Metro-Goldwyn-Mayer, or whether it was, as Clarke instead claimed, that HAL stands for **H**euristically programmed **AL**gorithmic computer. In any case, HAL was the AI that inspired me most as a young boy to devote my career to building intelligence in machines.

My other favourite robot in space was Marvin, the paranoid android from Douglas Adams' marvellous *The Hitchhiker's Guide to the Galaxy*. A few quotes from Marvin give you a good picture of his endearing personality.

"*Life!* Don't talk to me about life."

"I think you ought to know I'm feeling very depressed."

"I could calculate your chance of survival, but you won't like it."

"Here I am, brain the size of a planet and they ask me to take you down to the bridge. Call that *job satisfaction*? 'Cos I don't."

"Then of course I've got this terrible pain in all the diodes down my left-hand side . . ."

It's hard to know why Marvin is such a sympathetic character. Perhaps Marvin reflects our hopes and fears regarding AI and robotics? Will AI have to grapple with the same existential questions and emotional struggles that have troubled us humans? Or is it simply that intelligence and happiness are often difficult bedfellows? Whatever it is, Marvin is, in my view, one of the more enjoyable robotic creations ever imagined. And I can't wait for Marvin to be made not in our imagination but in silicon.

ROOMBA

I come now to perhaps the most popular robot on the planet today, the humble robot vacuum cleaner. Market leader iRobot claims to have sold more than 40 million Roomba vacuum cleaner robots globally. Given that iRobot has roughly a 50 per cent share of the robot vacuum cleaner market, this means that around 80 million robot vacuum cleaners have been sold worldwide in total. That's more than the population of the United Kingdom. And all thanks to a visionary Australian by the name of Rodney Brooks.*

Brooks was born in Adelaide in 1954, studied mathematics at Flinders University and did his PhD at Stanford University. He eventually held the prestigious position of Panasonic professor of robotics at the Massachusetts Institute of Technology (MIT) and served as director of the MIT Computer

---

* Again, I'm lucky enough to know Rodney Brooks well. Yes, AI is a small field and it's been a real privilege to have met most of the pioneers over the 40 years that I've been working in it.

Science and Artificial Intelligence Laboratory. But he wasn't just an academic interested in advancing research on AI and robotics. He wanted robots to have a real impact on people's lives. So, in 1990, he co-founded iRobot, a company with the goal of creating intelligent machines that could perform useful tasks in the real world.* In 2002, iRobot introduced the Roomba robot vacuum. This was the first practical home robot that could navigate around your home and help keep it clean.

The first Roomba robots were quite primitive. They included sensors to stop them bumping into furniture but didn't have any internal map of the space that they were vacuuming. They instead performed what mathematicians call a "drunkard's walk": whenever they met an obstacle, they turned at random and set off again in a new direction. This isn't as dumb it sounds. Such a random walk will eventually reach any accessible point in your home. Since 2015, however, Roomba robots have been able to create a map of your home. This means they can more efficiently vacuum, as well as return to the charger. And yes, that means your robot is spying on you. In fact, at the end of 2022, embarrassing images of people on the toilet taken by a Roomba J7 series robot vacuum ended up on Facebook after they were sent to Scale AI, a start-up that uses humans to label data for training artificial intelligence.

iRobot's robots aren't just limited to people's homes. They've explored the Great Pyramid of Giza for hidden chambers, defused bombs in Iraq and Afghanistan, gathered data

---

* A shout-out to the other two co-founders of iRobot, Colin Angle and Helen Greiner.

at the Fukushima nuclear disaster site and detected underwater oil spills after the 2010 Deepwater Horizon disaster.

Amazon's AU$2.5 billion takeover deal of iRobot, announced in August 2022, collapsed in January 2024 following scrutiny by the European Commission on antitrust grounds. Despite Amazon paying iRobot a termination fee of $94 million, the company announced it would have to lay off a third of its staff. I hope this is just a minor hiccup on its journey to bring more robots into our lives.

STANLEY

One other place that robots are entering our lives is on our roads. You might not think of it as a robot, but a self-driving car is, in fact, a robot.* A robot is a machine that has sensors to provide it with information about the world, a computer to make decisions and actuators to interact with the environment. A self-driving car has sensors like cameras to see the road, onboard computers to make decisions about where to drive, when to accelerate and when to brake, and actuators to change the throttle, activate the brakes and turn the steering wheel. That makes them robots.

No doubt you're complaining that we've been promised self-driving cars for many decades. As far back as 1940, in his book *Magic Motorways*, the industrial designer Norman Bel Geddes boldly imagined self-driving cars by 1960. More recently, Elon Musk has also predicted their imminent arrival.

---

* By the way, who is the self in a self-driving car?

In 2015, he said it would take about three years. In 2016, he upped the ante and promised we'd have self-driving cars one year earlier, by 2017. In 2019, the date slipped to 2020. And in 2022, he again promised it was just a year away. He was wrong every time.

So where are the self-driving cars? The reality is that they are arriving by stealth. Modern cars are essentially computers on wheels. You'll find them full of sensors like cameras, lidars and radars for sensing the world. And self-driving capabilities are now common for driving on the highway. Of course, the highway is an easier problem than the town: all the traffic is going the same way, and there are fewer challenges like cyclists, pedestrians or four-way stops to navigate. But self-driving cars are increasingly coping with these challenges too.

The technology to build self-driving cars has been many decades in development. In 2004, the US agency DARPA launched a million-dollar prize to stimulate research into self-driving cars. Fifteen teams competed for the prize on a 150-mile route (approximately 240 kilometres) across the Mojave Desert on the California–Nevada border. It was an abject failure. Two vehicles had to be withdrawn before the final race began. Another flipped upside down in the starting area. And after only a few hours of desert driving, most vehicles had suffered critical failures, leading to disqualification or withdrawal. The furthest any self-driving vehicle travelled was a pathetic seven of the 150 miles.

The following year, with twice the prize money at stake, teams did much better. Five of the 23 teams successfully completed the 132-mile desert course. The winner was Stanley from Stanford University, which completed the route in just under seven hours, a mere 11 minutes ahead of their great rival, Sandstorm from Carnegie Mellon University. Stanley might make you think of Stanford but was, in fact, named after Stanley Kubrick. The car was a heavily adapted 2005 Volkswagen Touareg that can now be seen at the National Air and Space Museum in Washington, D.C.* Sebastian Thrun, the leader of the winning team, said of the result: "The impossible has been achieved."

Stanley was another seemingly overnight success that was decades in the making. One of the earliest and most important precursors to Stanley was the Eureka PROMETHEUS project. This was funded by the European Union from 1987 to 1994, at a not insignificant cost of 800 million euros. The project brought together a consortium of European automakers, universities and tech companies to develop self-driving capabilities. When PROMETHEUS ended in 1994, the technologies and systems underwent real-world testing in two specially designed autonomous prototype vehicles – VaMP and VITA-2. In a landmark achievement, these self-driving cars successfully navigated over 1000 kilometres on highways circling Paris, in regular traffic, at speeds reaching 130 kilometres per hour. If you have ever driven on a French highway, you'll appreciate what a feat this was.

These prototypes demonstrated self-driving technologies – such as computer vision for lane sensing, radar-based collision

---

* You might wonder why a car is in an air and space museum. The reason is that Stanley used a GPS satellite navigation system.

avoidance and route planning – that are now commonplace. They were thus critical stepping stones paving the way for Stanley, and for the autonomous vehicles Waymo, Cruise, Tesla and others are building today.

SOPHIA

Let me end this brief intermission with one final robot that has caused a lot of concern among the public. This is Sophia, a very realistic humanoid robot that has amazed audiences at the United Nations, on TV and around the world. In fact, Sophia is so famous she has her own Wikipedia page. When Sophia was proclaimed a citizen of Saudi Arabia in October 2017, worry went viral. Were sentient robots arriving? Did robots now need rights? And let us not forget that the Kingdom of Saudi Arabia at that time gave conspicuously fewer rights to women than to this robot.

Sophia is not something you need to worry about. In reality, Sophia is a bit of a fraud. To understand the deceit, it helps to peer into the curious mind that brought Sophia into being: David Hanson Jr, the founder and CEO of Hanson Robotics. Hanson is a dreamer straddling the realms of art and science. He started out with a Bachelor of Fine Arts in film, then worked for Disney as an "imagineer", creating sculptures and animatronic figures for their theme parks, before getting his PhD in aesthetic studies. And he is obsessed with creating robots in human form. But his creations are more style than substance.

Hanson believes robots that closely resemble humans will be able to connect deeply and meaningfully with people. And the reaction of audiences when Sophia is demoed would seem to confirm this belief. Sophia appears beguilingly human. Crimson lips. Fluttering eye lashes and an admiring gaze that seems to track your movements. Sophia's sorcery is amplified by what appears to be a conversational spontaneity that toys with the boundaries of what is possible. In 2018, a member of the audience at the annual Brain Bar event in Budapest, a sort of South by Southwest on the Danube, asked Sophia about her first memory. Sophia responded: "Opening my eyes and coming online. The white walls and green cupboards of the lab. David's face."

When host Jimmy Fallon quipped about her lifelike appearance on *The Tonight Show* in 2017, Hanson supplied a subtle storyteller's nudge: "She is, basically, alive." This set off a firestorm. "Complete bullshit!" bellowed Yann LeCun,

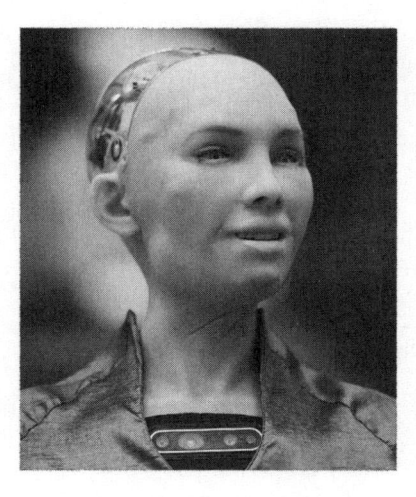

Sophia at the Global Media Forum in Bonn, 2019.

chief AI scientist for Facebook AI Research, on Twitter (now X), likening Sophia to "Cargo Cult AI", in which the superficial trappings of intelligence are mistaken for genuine cognitive capabilities, much to the chagrin of serious AI researchers.

LeCun has a point. Sophia is largely theatre, and has very little intelligence below the surface. Sophia's conversations and gestures are carefully scripted. Indeed, I once tried to hire Sophia to open a large AI conference. I was shocked by the AU$50,000 price tag to fly her into Melbourne for the day. But I wasn't surprised by the booking form, which laid out how pre-programmed her conversations would need to be. The deeper story is that Sophia plays on our natural human gullibility. We're quick to assign human values to inanimate objects when they appear human – even when there is little or no intelligence, artificial or otherwise, behind the facade.

All I can say is, you have been warned!

PART 2
THE LEARNING ERA

IDEA #4:

ARTIFICIAL BRAINS

WE MOVE NOW TO the second half of this shortest history of artificial intelligence.

So far, AI has been programmed. We thought carefully about how humans solve problems. We considered, for example, how humans navigated (Lesson #1: Searching for answers), played games (Lesson #2: Making the best move) or became an expert in a narrow domain (Lesson #3: Applying rules). And then we wrote AI programs to simulate these processes. But this approach of programming AI by hand is slow and painful. And it is also very dependent on our not-very-good human introspection about our own problem-solving. Surely there must be a better way?

Human intelligence again provides inspiration. We go to school to *learn* many of the intelligent things we do. We aren't born able to read, write, solve quadratic equations or compose sonnets. Most of the intelligent things we do are things we *learnt* to do. Could computers not also learn to do such things?

It's an idea first put forwards by Alan Turing in his 1950 paper, "Computing Machinery and Intelligence". As you will recall, this is generally considered to be the first scientific paper about artificial intelligence, in which Turing introduced his eponymous test for AI. However, it also introduced another very important idea. Having considered reasons why artificial intelligence might not be possible, Turing turned to the question of how we might actually build AI. And here he proposed the idea of "learning machines":

> Instead of trying to produce a programme to simulate the adult mind, why not rather try to produce one which simulates the child's? If this were then subjected to an appropriate course of education one would obtain the adult brain.

Despite the obvious attractions of Turing's idea, "learning machines" didn't get much traction in the early days of AI. Indeed, it was not till the 2010s that a new approach called "deep learning" was introduced, and "learning machines" dramatically took off.

Again, the "overnight" success of deep learning was more than 50 years in the making. And to understand this success, we must again go back to the Second World War, and meet two colourful characters from the early history of AI.

*

Learning happens in brains. A natural way to build a machine that learns would therefore be to build an artificial brain. Hence the fourth idea central to AI today: **You can copy the**

IDEA #4: ARTIFICIAL BRAINS

human brain with a network of artificial neurons that learn from experience.

There are just two small problems with this idea. The first problem is that the human brain is arguably the most complex object in the known universe. Nothing that we know approaches the complexity of the billions of neurons and the trillions of synapses that connect them. And the second problem is that we have very little idea of how even an individual neuron in the brain works, let alone billions of them. But these two small problems didn't stop our next two extraordinary individuals from trying to simulate a simple brain in a computer. Let me introduce Walter Pitts and Warren McCulloch, gifted and eccentric academics who, in the 1940s, laid the foundations for neural networks, one of the most important technologies so far developed in the history of AI.

Walter Pitts was a child prodigy from a tough Detroit home. According to legend, he ducked into the library one day to escape some neighbourhood bullies. He stayed there after closing, and for the next three days read *Principia Mathematica*, the text we came across earlier in connection to the Logic Theorist, the first AI program. *Principia Mathematica* is a 2000-page textbook that Bertrand Russell and Alfred Whitehead wrote to provide a logical foundation to all of mathematics. It is one of the most celebrated and important books on mathematics ever written. But this didn't stop the precocious Pitts from finding several mathematical errors in it. And so he wrote a letter to Bertrand Russell, pointing out these problems.

In reply, Russell generously invited Pitts to Cambridge University to study with him as one of his graduate students.

He hadn't realised that Pitts was only 12 years old. Unsurprisingly, Pitts did not take up Russell's offer. He did, however, continue to correspond with Bertrand Russell. Aged 15, he left home to hang around the University of Chicago, where he attended some lectures that Russell gave.

Chicago is also where Pitts fell into the orbit of Warren McCulloch, a professor of psychiatry at the neighbouring University of Illinois. McCulloch was from a very different background than the homeless Pitts. McCulloch was born into a well-off East Coast family of lawyers, doctors and engineers. He had attended Yale and Columbia, and years of privilege had produced a confident, chain-smoking academic who was part philosopher, part poet and part scientist.

Walter Pitts (left) and Warren McCulloch (photographed by Lotfi Zadeh, the father of fuzzy logic).

IDEA #4: ARTIFICIAL BRAINS

The one thing that this unlikely couple, Pitts and McCulloch, had in common was the legendary Gottfried Leibniz. They both worshipped the 17th-century philosopher, especially his attempt to create an alphabet of human thought that was, as I discussed earlier, part of the prehistory of AI. And so, together, Pitts and McCulloch set about continuing Leibniz's work.

Principia Mathematica was their other inspiration. Russell and Whitehead reduced all of mathematics to a simple logic of true and false, or 1 and 0, combining true (1) and false (0) with conjunction ("and"), disjunction ("or") and negation ("not"). Pitts and McCulloch looked to repeat this binary decomposition with their simplified model of an artificial brain.

The brain is a binary device in which neurons fire or they don't. And these neurons are connected in the brain in a complex network. So Pitts and McCulloch's idea was to decompose an artificial brain into a simple network of binary neurons, similar to how a logical formula might be decomposed using simple logical connectives like "AND", "OR" and "NOT".

AN ARTIFICIAL NEURON

Pitts and McCulloch began with a simple binary model of a neuron called the "perceptron". This is, in essence, a logical gate. It has two or more inputs. The perceptron adds up a weighted sum of these inputs. If the sum exceeds a threshold, then the output of the perceptron fires. If the sum does not exceed the threshold, then the output does not fire. This explains how a perceptron works. But how does it learn?

This is where the weights on the inputs to the perceptron come in. Just as learning in the brain strengthens or weakens the input to the brain's neurons, we simply adjust the weights to the inputs to the perceptron. More important inputs to the perceptron get larger weights, while less important inputs get smaller weights.

We could adjust weights at random until we find a good combination. But there's a more systematic way where we slowly increase or decrease weights. And Frank Rosenblatt, a psychology lecturer at Cornell University, went about implementing this, first in 1957 in software on an IBM 704 computer, and later in 1960 in hardware. The Mark 1 Perceptron that he built was the first neural network. It now resides at the Smithsonian Institution.

The Mark 1 Perceptron was an "artificial brain". And it caught the public's imagination. The *New York Times* reported the perceptron to be "the embryo of an electronic computer that it [the Navy funding the research] expects will be able to walk, talk, see, write, reproduce itself and be conscious of its existence".[1] Rosenblatt fuelled these grandiose hopes with grand claims. In 1958, he wrote:

> Stories about the creation of machines having human qualities have long been a fascinating province in the realm of science fiction. Yet we are about to witness the birth of such a machine – a machine capable of perceiving, recognizing and identifying its surroundings without any human training or control.[2]

There were reasons for optimism (though perhaps not for quite this much optimism): initial results with the Mark 1 Perceptron did look promising. And it had been shown that a network of perceptrons could, in theory, implement *any* logical function. But reality soon came crashing down. After all, a simple network of perceptrons is a grossly simplified model of the human brain. It was even a grossly simplified model of the limited understanding of the human brain that scientists had in the 1940s. In the human brain, for example, connections can be both created and destroyed, while the network of the perceptron was fixed. And neurons are affected by the timing of incoming signals, while perceptrons work synchronously.

These simplifications were, however, not the reason that perceptrons would become deeply unfashionable. Rosenblatt ran into some strong opposition that set back the field of neural networks by decades. In particular, several key researchers vocally turned against the idea of the perceptron – perhaps none more important than Marvin Minsky, one of the organisers of the Dartmouth workshop and a leading figure in AI. A now-famous book titled *Perceptrons*, written by Minsky and Seymour Papert, both from MIT, was published in 1969. The book explored the limits of what you could compute with perceptrons. Perhaps most significantly of all, the book showed it was impossible for a network with a single layer of perceptrons to learn a concept as simple as "even or odd".

Their book shouldn't have had the negative impact that it did have. It turns out that if you go beyond a *single* layer to a network of perceptrons with *multiple* layers, then perceptrons can indeed learn a concept like "even or odd". But the idea that perceptrons were somewhat limited stuck.

Others have suggested that perceptrons fell out of favour around this time as Rosenblatt's perceptron learning rule was just too slow. (It would take till the 2010s and three major advances – the popularisation of the backpropagation rule for learning, as well as much faster computers and larger training datasets – for this problem to be fixed.) Or it may have been the ongoing battle between the two camps – those in favour of symbolic AI and those committed to machine learning. Fans of the symbolic approach to AI, such as John McCarthy and Marvin Minsky, were in influential positions by the late 1960s. And while Frank Rosenblatt had a forceful personality, his overly enthusiastic claims didn't help his cause.

Whatever it was, the wind was knocked out of the sails of the neural network revolution for the next 40 years. Rosenblatt continued working on perceptrons despite significantly diminished funding. But many others didn't. Indeed, many left the field completely and neural networks became deeply unfashionable. His last attempt to use perceptrons was a speech recognition system called Tobermory, built between 1961 and 1967. This was a perceptron network with four layers and 12,000 weights implemented by toroidal magnetic cores. Tobermory occupied an entire room, but such impressive hardware was already easily outperformed by the general-purpose digital computers of the day. Rosenblatt's specialised hardware had been left behind by Moore's law, the exponential improvements that have powered the computing revolution.

> Frank Rosenblatt was a fascinating character with interests that ranged from astronomy to music, mountaineering and politics. He attended the Bronx High School of Science, a school that has produced more Nobel Prize winners than any other, as well as educating several Turing Award winners, including Marvin Minsky. In later life, Rosenblatt built an observatory on a hilltop near to his house which he used to search for extraterrestrial intelligence. Sadly, he drowned in a boating accident in 1971 on his 43rd birthday.* By this time, Rosenblatt had moved on from the perceptron and his research now involved injecting material from trained rats' brains into the brains of untrained rats to see if the untrained rats would become smarter.

DEEP LEARNING

Frank Rosenblatt's dreams didn't die out completely with the publication of Minsky and Papert's book. One pioneering AI researcher, Geoff Hinton, continued Rosenblatt's mission to build an artificial brain. Indeed, Hinton systematically went about addressing the problems the book had raised.

Geoff Hinton – or, to give him his full name, Geoffrey Everest Hinton – is the great-great-grandson of George Boole. You will remember George Boole appeared in the short prehistory of AI as the inventor of Boolean logic, the logic of 0s and 1s that computers use today. And Hinton's middle name comes from another historic relative, Sir George Everest,

---

* I'm not sure why the history of AI features quite so many untimely deaths, but it does.

the surveyor-general of India, after whom the mountain is named.

In 2015, I attended the bicentenary celebrations of George Boole's birth at his alma mater, Queen's College, Cork (now University College Cork). Geoff Hinton was also there, as were several other of Boole's descendants. The strong family genetics were impossible to ignore.

Throughout his career, Geoff Hinton has been a maverick, unafraid to pursue the unconventional and the unfashionable, just like his great-great-grandfather did 200 years before him. In Hinton's case, he doggedly developed neural networks for many decades, from the late 1970s onwards, despite the area being deeply unfashionable and despite strong resistance from the scientific community.

As an undergraduate at the University of Cambridge, Hinton had struggled to find an intellectual home. He tried his hand at many things. He studied natural sciences, the history of art and then philosophy before finally settling on

George Boole (left) and his great-great-grandson Geoff Hinton.

experimental psychology. He continued with postgraduate studies at the department of artificial intelligence at the University of Edinburgh. At that time, Edinburgh had the only department of artificial intelligence in the world. He was awarded a PhD in computer vision from Edinburgh in 1977.*

Hinton was unable to find funding in the United Kingdom for his unpopular ideas about AI, so he moved first to the United States, where he worked briefly at the University of California San Diego and then Carnegie Mellon University, before washing up in Canada at the University of Toronto. There he found support from a far-sighted but little-known funding agency, the Canadian Institute for Advanced Research (CIFAR).

The first issue that was thought to plague perceptrons, as we have seen, was their inability to learn even simple concepts like "even or odd". Hinton quickly showed that an additional intermediate (or, as it is often called, "hidden") layer of neurons allows neural networks to learn "even or odd" and other, more complicated, functions. Hinton didn't, however, stop with just *one extra* layer but instead popularised the idea of "deep learning", using neural networks with *many* layers.

The next issue that Hinton needed to address was the speed of this learning. In 1986, with David Rumelhart and Ronald J. Williams, Hinton wrote a very influential paper that promoted a much faster learning rule for updating the weights in neural networks. The rule was called "backpropagation". Backpropagation wasn't "invented" by a single person. The term

---

* I was lucky enough to get my PhD from this same department, one decade after Hinton.

itself was coined by Rosenblatt in 1962, but he didn't know how to implement it. Some credit might be given to Paul Werbos, who proposed training neural networks with backpropagation in 1982, but he was preceded by Seppo Linnainmaa in 1970. Many others also deserve credit, including Arthur E. Bryson (1961), Henry J. Kelley (1960) and Lev Pontryagin (late 1950s). In fact, backpropagation is essentially an application of the chain rule for differentiation, which many of us learnt at school, and which was invented by Gottfried Leibniz, another character from our short prehistory of AI, back in 1673.

Backpropagation is a smart way to update the weights in a neural network. It computes a gradient – the rate at which the output changes as the input changes. And just like you can more quickly climb a mountain by following the steepest slope, backpropagation follows the gradient to find the best weights more quickly. Backpropagation meant that the weights in a deep network with many layers could be learnt faster. But the computations to do so were still rather onerous.

A chance discovery in 2012 by one of Hinton's PhD students, Alex Krizhevsky, provided a means to perform backpropagation even more efficiently. Alex realised that GPUs, the graphic processors used to render 3D video in computer games, were ideally suited to perform the matrix calculations needed to compute gradients and do backpropagation. This meant Hinton now had an efficient way to train very deep neural networks.

The discovery would quickly add over a trillion US dollars to the market capitalisation of NVIDIA Corporation, the company with an 80 per cent share of the GPU market. They are surely one of the luckiest companies ever. They found themselves, by chance, selling the shovels for the AI revolution.

A RECIPE FOR LEARNING

Geoff Hinton had identified backpropagation as a better learning algorithm for neural networks. He also had much more efficient computing power to do backpropagation, thanks to GPUs. These two ingredients meant neural networks could now be a lot deeper. The deep learning recipe – backpropagation over deep neural networks using GPUs to manage the computational load – was almost complete. Hinton just needed the third and final ingredient to get deep learning to work well. That final ingredient was training data. Lots of it. Machine learning methods such as deep learning need massive amounts of training data. Ideally hundreds of thousands or even millions of examples from which to learn. Humans don't need so many examples to learn so it was perhaps understandable that previous attempts to build neural networks just hadn't trained on enough data to get good results.

Fortunately for Hinton, another AI researcher by the name of Fei-Fei Li had come to the same conclusion in 2006. And she had been working hard to fix it. Her focus was computer vision, specifically object recognition. Could you get a computer to identify objects in an image? *That's an apple. That's a banana. That's a bicycle. That's a person.* Object recognition is an important task in a range of applications, from fruit picking to self-driving cars. She therefore set about building ImageNet, a large database of training examples for computer vision algorithms.

Fei-Fei Li grew up in Chengdu, an industrial city in southern China and immigrated to the United States with her family at 15. They had little money, but she got a scholarship to Princeton, then undertook a doctorate at Caltech in Pasadena, working at the intersection of neuroscience and computer science. In 2007, she moved back to Princeton University as an assistant professor. She then became director of the legendary Stanford Artificial Intelligence Lab, and, during a sabbatical from Stanford, chief AI scientist at Google Cloud.

In 2007, Li began the task of building ImageNet by paying students $10 an hour to label images to include in her database. But progress was slow and expensive. Then a student suggested she try the crowdsourcing service Amazon Mechanical Turk. Now she could hire many workers, and (somewhat controversially) it would only cost a fraction of what she was paying the Princeton students.

Fei-Fei Li at the AI for Good Global Summit in Geneva, 2017.

By 2009, ImageNet had over 3 million images and was released to the world. It has since grown to over 14 million images, all helpfully labelled into one of 21,000 categories such as "balloon", "banana" or "boat". And then, to promote ImageNet in particular and AI research in general, an annual competition called the ImageNet Large Scale Visual Recognition Challenge began in 2010. This pitted the best computer vision algorithms in the world against each other. The competition was a great success, focusing the research community's attention and accelerating progress in AI.

In the 2012 ImageNet competition, Geoff Hinton, Alex Krizhevsky and Ilya Sutskever, another of Hinton's PhD students, put all three ingredients for deep learning together for the first time: backpropagation over a deep network, computation using GPUs and lots of training data. Their simple recipe worked a treat; indeed, their entry blew the opposition out of the water. The eight-layer deep learning network they built, AlexNet, had an error rate of just 15.3 per cent, beating the runner-up by more than 10.8 percentage points. This remains the largest winning margin in the competition's history.

Interestingly, AlexNet wasn't the first deep neural network, or the first GPU-powered deep neural network, or even the first GPU-powered deep neural network, to win a competition by a large margin. Yann LeCun is now chief AI scientist at Meta and a professor at New York University. But back in 1995, he and some of his colleagues at Bell Labs in New Jersey had a pioneering seven-layer neural network called LeNet-5. This was deployed by companies like NCR to read over 10 per cent of bank cheques in the United States during the late 1990s and early 2000s. It was also used by the US Postal Service to help sort letters by recognising the digits in zip codes on handwritten letters. Various other researchers had also used GPUs to speed up neural networks since at least 2006. And Jürgen Schmidhuber's DanNet, a GPU-powered deep neural network, had already won four computer vision competitions in a row in 2011 and 2012, in some cases by impressive margins.[3]

But it was AlexNet that put all three ingredients together and caught the attention of AI researchers around the world. It announced, with a big bang, the start of the deep learning revolution. And the echo of that bang can still be heard today in AI systems like ChatGPT from OpenAI and Gemini from Google.

In the northern-hemisphere autumn of 2012, Hinton, Krizhevsky and Sutskever founded a start-up company to capitalise on their recipe for **d**eep **n**eural **n**etwork **research** called DNNResearch. Just a few months later, in December 2012, at the main conference for neural network research at Harrah's and Harvey's Casino on Lake Tahoe, Hinton decided to cash out. He organised an auction of DNNResearch, inviting Google, Microsoft, Baidu and DeepMind (which was yet to be bought by Google) to bid. Hinton stopped the auction when Google bid $44 million. He could have undoubtably got more, but this was, he felt, a fair price for a company with just three employees (the three founders), no products and half-a-dozen patents to its name.

As part of the acquisition, Hinton, Krizhevsky and Sutskever all went to work for Google. Three years later, in December 2015, Sutskever would leave Google to co-found and become chief scientist at OpenAI, a company we will discuss shortly, as it has played an outsized role in the recent history of AI. Krizhevsky would also leave Google for a deep-learning start-up in September 2017. This start-up was acquired by Square in 2020. Hinton, on the other hand, stayed at Google till he retired in 2023.

TRANSFORMERS
To get to AI chatbots like ChatGPT and many of the more recent advances in AI being pushed forwards by companies like Google, Meta and OpenAI, we still need two more important ingredients. The first ingredient is the "T" in "GPT". This stands for "transformer", which is a particular architecture for connecting the neurons in a neural network. Think of it as a wiring diagram for neural networks that works especially well with sequential data. Sequential data is any data, like text, that occurs in sequence, and where the order matters. And sequential data covers a lot of useful cases besides text, such as weather data, stock prices, protein sequences, music and speech.

Going back to AlexNet in 2012, that was a computer vision system, designed to process images. Images are not sequential or one-dimensional, but two-dimensional. This two-dimensionality is important to take into account when processing images. For example, you can shift an image left or right, up or down, and the image doesn't essentially change. A banana remains a banana, even if you move it two pixels to the left or three pixels down.

To take advantage of the two-dimensional nature of images, neural networks like AlexNet use a particular architecture called a convolutional neural network. This architecture lets the neural network deal with shifted images. In particular, a convolutional neural network looks for changes in pixels rather than for particular pixels. This works well with processing two-dimensional images. Such an architecture isn't much good for processing data such as text, which is not two-dimensional. Text is a one-dimensional sequence of words. In fact, with text, we can be interested in features that might be a long distance apart. Local changes may not matter much. Consider a sentence like the following:

> Alice knew that her work contained errors but she wasn't going to point them out.

The pronoun "them" refers to the noun "errors", while the pronoun "she" refers to the noun "Alice". Both pronouns are a long way away from the nouns to which they refer. This is where the transformer architecture has an important role to play. It allows neural networks to identify such long-range dependencies using a mechanism called attention.

It should not come as a surprise that we might need different neural architectures for different tasks. We know this already from the human brain. Speech and language are processed in the frontal and temporal lobes, while vision is processed in the visual cortex. And these different areas of the brain have different neural structures.

The transformer architecture was first proposed in 2017 by a team at Google Research in a famous paper called "Attention Is All You Need".[4] This paper has since become a classic, with

IDEA #4: ARTIFICIAL BRAINS

over 100,000 citations. This makes it the fourth most cited paper in the whole of scientific literature. Transformers are now used in a wide range of AI systems that process sequential one-dimensional data, from Google Translate through to OpenAI's chatbot ChatGPT, Zoom's audio transcription service and even Descript's voice-cloning software. Transformers are one of the main reasons for the most recent AI boom. And remarkably, Google gave transformers away by openly publishing the idea of the transformer architecture in the scientific literature in 2017 for all to use freely.

> The title of the Google Research team's famous paper on transformer architecture is a playful nod to the Beatles hit song "All You Need Is Love". This song is also rather historic, as it was written for the first live global television show on 25 June 1967. This beamed out its message of love, via satellite, to an audience of over 400 million people in 25 countries around the world. A copy of the lyrics to the song in Lennon's handwriting sold at auction for $1.25 million in 2005.

As their name suggests, transformers transform: they change complex inputs into complex outputs. For example, they can transform:

- a sequence of words in one language into an equivalent sequence in another language, as they do in Google Translate;

- a sequence of words into a picture, as they do in DALL-E;
- a sequence of words representing a question into another sequence of words representing the answer to that question, as they do in ChatGPT;
- an audio sequence into a sequence of words that is a transcription of that audio, as they do in the Zoom speech-to-text transcription tool.

There are four parts to a transformer. You can think of the input data flowing through the four parts in turn, being transformed at each part into different forms. We start with the input. Suppose this is a sequence of words. The first transformation is to turn this into something that a computer can process: a sequence of numbers. This first step is called tokenisation. There are more than a million words in English, so it would be prohibitive to have a separate number for each one. Therefore, tokenisation replaces common words with individual numbers (called tokens), but breaks down more complex words into parts, each of which is represented by a token. A typical transformer uses between 50,000 and 200,000 different tokens.

Consider a sentence like, "The secret of success is to do the common thing uncommonly well." This is broken into the following words and word parts: "the", "secret", "of", "success", "is", "to", "do", "the", "common", "thing", "un", "commonly", "well". Note how an uncommon word like "uncommonly" is broken into the two more common parts: "un" and "commonly". Each word or word part is then replaced by a number.

This gives us a sequence of tokens: 24782, 14939, 38567, 4368, 48251, 28573, 36529, 45547, 7243, 13900, 33811, 19973, 49084. This sequence of numbers is something a neural network can easily act upon.

WORD VECTORS

So far, the transformer has transformed text into a sequence of numbers. Numbers are good; computers are excellent at manipulating numbers. But we've lost something in this transformation of text into a sequence of numbers. We've lost the complex relationships that exist between words. A word like "queen" is near to a word like "king". "Queen" is also near to a word like "bee". And while a word like "beetle" is also near to "bee", "beetle" is not very near to "queen". This creates a headache when building AI to deal with language. There's no way to choose numbers so the token for the word "queen" is close numerically to that for "bee", and the token for "bee" is near to that for "beetle", but the token for the "beetle" is numerically far from that for "queen".

The solution to this problem is to transform numbers into something less one dimensional. Thus, the second step in a transformer maps these tokens onto a more complex representation called a vector, which can capture complex relationships. A number is a point on a one-dimensional line. A vector is simply a point in a multi-dimensional space. And in this case, I'm not talking about the usual two- or three-dimensional space you're used to visualising. I'm talking about a vector with hundreds or even thousands of dimensions. Now, it's very hard to imagine more than three dimensions. Geoff Hinton often gives the advice that to imagine fourteen dimensions, you imagine three dimensions, and repeatedly say to yourself loudly, "Fourteen." I'm afraid that I can't offer you a better trick.

This step – turning tokens into vectors of numbers – is called encoding. And by turning words into vectors of numbers, we can capture the complex relationships between words. Let me illustrate with three dimensions. But remember, we have hundreds or even thousands of dimensions to play with, and to capture even more complex relationships between words.

Suppose the word "queen" gets transformed into the vector [0.5, 0.3, -0.2]. And "king" is transformed into the vector [0.7, 0.5, -0.4]. Similarly, suppose the word "man" is transformed into the vector [0.6, 0.4, -0.3]. And "woman" becomes the vector [0.4, 0.2, -0.1]. Let's take "queen", or [0.5, 0.3, -0.2]. Now subtract "woman" from it, component-wise. This gives us [0.5, 0.3, -0.2] – [0.4, 0.2, -0.1] which equals the vector [0.1, 0.1, -0.1]. Now let's add "man" to this vector component-wise, [0.1, 0.1, -0.1] + [0.6, 0.4, -0.3]. This equals [0.7, 0.5, -0.4]. Cutely, this is the vector for "king". Thus we have shown mathematically that in this multidimensional space of vectors:

King = Queen + (man – woman)

Such a vector encoding creates its own challenges. For example, it has been shown that encoding can create sexist vector equations such as:

computer programmer + (woman – man)
= homemaker

And:

architect + (woman − man) = hairdresser

This reflects sexism in the text on which the encoder is trained.[5] It is clearly undesirable. And if we work harder, sexism (and other unwanted biases) in word vectors can be fixed.

To recap, the first step is tokenisation, transforming words into a sequence of tokens. The second step is encoding, which transforms a sequence of tokens into a sequence of word vectors. The third step in a transformer is where even more magic happens. So far, the transformer has tried to capture the meaning of words by mapping them onto vectors in a high-dimension space. But we haven't taken account of connections between words in a body of text. In the third step, the transformer uncovers relationships between words.

Let's go back to our example sentence:

Alice knew that her work contained errors but she wasn't going to point them out.

After encoding, the vectors for "she" and "them" are generic. They're the same vectors in any sentence containing "she" and "them". In the third step, the attention mechanism modifies the vectors so that the vector for "she" is close to that for "Alice", and the vector for "them" is close to that for "errors". It thereby identifies the pronoun referents.

This step also resolves homonyms (words with the same spelling but different meanings) and polysemy (words with multiple related meanings). Is it a *river bank* or a *money bank*? And is this *dish* a *meal* or a *plate*?

The fourth and final step is decoding. This transforms vectors back into tokens. If the decoder simply inverts the encoder, then we obtain another English sentence. But if the decoder is for Russian, then we can obtain a Russian translation of the English sentence.

One of the most widely used AI systems built using transformers was BERT. This was proposed by researchers in Google in October 2018.[6] A year later, Google announced that they had started using BERT models to answer English-language search queries in the United States. Today, search queries on Google in over 70 different languages are processed by a BERT model. Many other AI models which, like BERT, use transformers to transform vectors of words have since been developed and named after characters in *Sesame Street*. Baidu's chatbot is, for example, called ERNIE, while Allen AI has made an encoder called ELMo. And there is a transformer-based fake-news detector called GROVER.

These *Sesame Street* names may be cute, but cuter still is that we can reduce so much of language simply to neural networks that transform vectors of numbers representing words. Who would have imagined that transforming vectors of numbers was all you needed to do to understand language?

GENERAL PURPOSE TECHNOLOGIES
Now that we have got to the arrival of *Sesame Street* characters, it is time to introduce OpenAI into the history. This company took the last two ideas – transformers and systems like

IDEA #4: ARTIFICIAL BRAINS

BERT – and pushed them aggressively. This caused a considerable leap in what AI systems could do.

OpenAI was founded as a not-for-profit venture in December 2015. The founders included Tesla CEO Elon Musk (who has since parted with the company and formed a rival company, xAI), Sam Altman (the current CEO of OpenAI), Greg Brockman (the current president) and Ilya Sutskever (who was the chief scientist, but has also left to form a rival company, Safe Superintelligence).

OpenAI has an ambitious mission: to "advance digital intelligence in the way that is most likely to benefit humanity as a whole, unconstrained by a need to generate financial return". Musk has previously spoken about his fears that the big tech companies were going to capture all the benefits of advanced AI. OpenAI was his hope of preventing this from happening.

Sam Altman, the charismatic and controversial CEO of OpenAI, in 2019.

The initial team behind OpenAI was stellar. Sutskever brought one of the strongest possible technical backgrounds in AI to the company. And Altman was a perfect choice to complement this. His previous job was running Silicon Valley's most important incubator, Y Combinator, making him an expert at scaling start-ups. And, as we shall see, scaling was what AI needed most of all.

When it was first set up, Musk was the largest backer of OpenAI. He put in somewhere between US$50 million and $100 million, of a total initial funding of around $130 million. Reid Hoffman, Peter Thiel and some other high-profile Silicon Valley backers also pledged over $1 billion to OpenAI, though it is far from clear if these pledges have ever been paid.

Scaling soon started eating into this seed funding. It became apparent that, while $1 billion was a huge amount of funding for a start-up with only a few hundred employees, it wasn't going to be enough to achieve OpenAI's goals. In March 2019, OpenAI therefore pivoted to a dual profit/non-profit status, and took what is currently over US$13 billion in investment from Microsoft.

In its first few years of operation, OpenAI struggled to achieve outcomes that matched the track records of its stellar team, as well as their considerable ambitions. Initial focus at OpenAI was on reinforcement learning, the topic of the next chapter. This was an obvious bet, given the success that others had been having with reinforcement learning in the previous couple of years. Indeed, OpenAI's first breakthrough was using reinforcement learning to defeat a world champion at Dota 2, a complex and very popular multiplayer video game, in which competition prize pools can reach over US$40 million.

Despite this initial success, OpenAI was operating somewhat in the shadow of DeepMind, a company with a five-year head start over OpenAI, and one that had been pioneering the use of reinforcement learning since 2010. (We'll come to DeepMind in the next chapter.) OpenAI also invested in some other areas such as robotics, but these ventures proved something of a failure. OpenAI quietly disbanded its robotics research team in 2021.

In 2018, this all changed and OpenAI hit gold. Its team took the ideas about transformers developed at Google with systems like BERT and scaled them aggressively with their GPT family of large language models – neural networks trained on vast troves of text. By using much more data and computation, they were able to build neural models with remarkable capabilities. Scaling aggressively was a risky gamble. To date, OpenAI has spent over $100 million training large language models. But this gamble has paid off a thousandfold – OpenAI is now worth around $100 billion.

OpenAI's first large language model in the GPT family, released in June 2018, was called GPT-1. The neural network has an impressive 17 million weights (or, as they are often called, parameters). This made it a large model at the time, but now it would be considered tiny. GPT-1 was trained on the Toronto Book Corpus, a dataset containing the text of around 7000 self-published books scraped from the internet. While the performance of GPT-1 was somewhat limited, it demonstrated that building larger models than those constructed by Google unlocked new capabilities.

> The Toronto Book Corpus is one of the few datasets scraped from the internet and used for training AI models that has not attracted public complaints from the owners of the copyrighted data. Self-published authors are, however, a rather specialised group. Many other authors have complained vocally about their work being used without consent or compensation – myself among them, as my books were included in the training set for GPT-3. There's a reason that OpenAI and other tech companies have used non-fiction books like mine to train their large language models. If you want a chatbot to be able to answer questions about everything from artificial intelligence to zoology, you need to train them on up-to-date content on everything from artificial intelligence to zoology.

Inspired by this promising outcome, OpenAI decided to go bigger still. Its second model in the GPT family, GPT-2, was released in February 2019. It was two orders of magnitude bigger than GPT-1, with 1.5 billion parameters. It was trained on a dataset of 8 million web pages, also more than an order of magnitude bigger than the dataset used with GPT-1. GPT-2 performed significantly better than GPT-1.

At this point, scale became everything in OpenAI's playbook. Their third model, GPT-3, was released in June 2020. It was two orders of magnitude bigger than GPT-2, with 175 billion parameters, and was trained on over half a trillion tokens scraped from the internet. The training data includes Wikipedia, Reddit and the contents of thousands of copyrighted books. The dataset was about 45 terabytes large, 500 times bigger than that used to train GPT-2. GPT-3 cost about

$5 million to train. The performance of GPT-3 surprised and excited many in the field.

OpenAI's fourth model, GPT-4, was released in March 2023. For commercial reasons, OpenAI is no longer very open about details, so we aren't exactly sure about the size of the model. Indeed, the only thing open about OpenAI now is its name. It is believed that GPT-4 has about 1.76 trillion parameters, and was trained on roughly 13 trillion tokens. In an interview, Altman claimed that GPT-4 had cost over $100 million to train.

As the GPT models got ever larger, their performance continued to improve. This is unusual in AI: we're used to running into combinatorial bottlenecks. We're used to scale making problems worse, not solving our problems. On the standard General Language Understanding Evaluation (the GLUE benchmark), which covers a wide range of language tasks such as sentence similarity, sentiment analysis and question answering, GPT-1 scored 70 per cent. Going bigger helped: GPT-2 scored 80 per cent, while GPT-3 reached an impressive 89 per cent. Even more impressively, the larger GPT models were able to do tasks – such as summarising text, writing computer code and translating between languages – that the models weren't explicitly trained to do.

GPT stands for **G**enerative **P**re-trained **T**ransformer. It is an ugly name. "Generative" means that the model can generate text. "Pre-trained" means that the model is pre-trained with no particular goal in mind other than to discover features in the training data. In this case, the model develops a general understanding of language, and is then finetuned for specific tasks such as answering questions, translating text or finishing sentences. And "Transformer" is because the model has a transformer architecture.

I suspect that OpenAI also chose the name GPT to remind us that they are trying to build a **g**eneral-**p**urpose **t**echnology. General-purpose technologies is a technical term in economics used to describe a technology that impacts a whole economy, with wide-ranging financial and societal consequences. Think technologies like the steam engine or electricity. "GPT" should therefore remind you that OpenAI is going after AGI, or artificial general intelligence. That's AI that matches human intelligence in all its capabilities. And there are many researchers at OpenAI, and within the AI field more broadly, who believe AGI will be achieved simply by scaling to larger GPTs. Whether that would need to be GPT-5 or GPT-15 is unclear. But whatever it is, I'll discuss shortly why such people might be wrong.

In November 2022, OpenAI made a master move and built a chatbot called ChatGPT on top of the GPT family. ChatGPT, which stands for "Chatting with GPT", finetuned the best GPT model of the time, GPT-3, to answer users' questions. While GPT-3 had caught the attention of the AI research community, ChatGPT captured the imagination of the world. It became the fastest-growing app ever. It had 1 million users after the first week, 100 million after the second month. And a year after its launch, it was available to over a billion people, with ChatGPT available through Microsoft's Bing search, as well as in WhatsApp, Skype and Snapchat.

Financially, ChatGPT was a massive success too. The value

of OpenAI increased a hundredfold, to around $100 billion. The company now has an annualised revenue of over $1 billion. We have never, in the long history of capitalism, seen wealth generated at such a rate. Even its strange capped for-profit status, which limits investors to 100 times return on their investment, hasn't held back the financial success of the company.

To build ChatGPT, OpenAI developed a novel type of reinforcement learning to finetune GPT models. I will cover this in the next chapter, where I discuss reinforcement learning in more detail. The result is a language model focused on doing whatever the user asks. This final ingredient created a neural network that ignited the public's interest.

I've already given a few examples of ChatGPT in action in earlier chapters of this book, but let me give you some more examples of its remarkable capabilities.

> **ME**: Write a sonnet in the style of William Shakespeare about the history of AI.
> **CHATGPT**:
> In days of yore, when minds with wonder teemed,
> To forge from thought a being of machine,
> Six seeds of AI, like stars in darkness gleamed,
> Their birth, a tale of intellect unseen.
>
> From ancient dreams to modern silicon's rise,
> In myths and quests, AI's roots were sown,
> Through symbolic eras, minds did devise,
> A mathematician in circuits known.

With rules to follow, expert systems grew,
Yet limits loomed, unseen by human eye,
The learning era dawned, a sky so blue,
With brains of artifice that dared to fly.

Now, in the future's gaze, we stand and see,
What wonders and what perils AI may be.

ME: Write one paragraph about the future history of AI.
CHATGPT: In the future history of AI, the 21st century will be remembered as the era when artificial intelligence transcended its limitations, reshaping every facet of human existence. Breakthroughs in deep learning and neural network architectures fueled an explosion of AI applications, revolutionizing industries from healthcare to finance, transportation to entertainment. As AI became increasingly integrated into daily life, society grappled with ethical dilemmas surrounding privacy, bias, and job displacement, prompting the establishment of international regulations and guidelines for responsible AI development. Despite challenges, the promise of AI to enhance human capabilities, drive innovation, and address pressing global challenges remained a driving force, propelling humanity towards a future where man and machine collaborated synergistically to unlock new frontiers of knowledge and possibility.

Very impressive, I think you'll agree? But how does it do such magic?

The overall idea behind ChatGPT is simple. It's like autocomplete on your phone, but on steroids. In the case of auto-complete, your phone has a dictionary of words and their frequencies. If you type the letters "APP", then auto-complete tells you that the most likely way to finish this word is "APPLE". ChatGPT just takes this further. It is trained not on a dictionary of words but on a significant fraction of the web. This scale means that ChatGPT can finish not just the word but also the sentence – even the paragraph or page.

This description of large language models like ChatGPT as auto-complete on steroids exposes a fundamental limitation. Such models are statistical. They're not *understanding* language like you or I do. They have no underlying model of the world.

Because they're not saying what is true but what is probable, large language models struggle most with reasoning. It's easy, therefore, to demonstrate their limitations. And these limitations are unlikely to disappear by simply scaling to bigger and bigger models. We will need some extra magic.

> **ME**: Limit everything you say to words that contain a single vowel.
> **CHATGPT**: Sure thing! This might get tricky, but I'll do my best. Ask away!
> **ME**: But "away" contains two vowels.
> **CHATGPT**: You're right! Let me try again. Feel free to ask!
> **ME**: "again", "feel" and "free" all contain two vowels.
> **CHATGPT**: Got it. I'll stick to single vowels. What's up?
> **ME**: But "vowels" contains two vowels.
> **CHATGPT**: True! I'll just stick to one vowel from now on. What's next?

One of the other major limitations of large language models like ChatGPT is that they make stuff up. People working in AI call this "hallucination", though this word choice is somewhat misleading: hallucination implies that the model actually knows the truth. The model has no knowledge of what is true or false. It merely says what is probable. What is remarkable is how often what is probable happens to be true.

Hallucination means large language models can generate misinformation and disinformation at speed and scale. It means they can and will be used as weapons of mass persuasion in political and other campaigns. This will trouble society greatly in the next decade or so. It's not hard to observe ChatGPT making stuff up. Note that if you try this at home, you might get a different answer as ChatGPT produces slightly different answers every time.

> **ME**: What was the first elephant to swim across the English channel?
>
> **CHATGPT**: The first elephant to swim across the English Channel was called "Jumbo." Jumbo was an African elephant who gained fame in the 19th century as part of P.T. Barnum's circus. In 1882, Jumbo, along with his companion Alice the elephant, swam across the English Channel from France to England as part of a publicity stunt organized by Barnum. The event garnered significant attention and further solidified Jumbo's status as a cultural icon.

For the record, Jumbo was a famous elephant from the London Zoo sold to the American entertainer Phineas T. Barnum in

IDEA #4: ARTIFICIAL BRAINS

1882. An elephant swimming the English Channel would surely have received a lot of media attention and would have been recorded by the newspapers. I searched the complete archive of the *New York Times*, the newspaper of record, and there is no record of any elephant ever swimming the Channel.

Here's another example of ChatGPT making stuff up.

ME: Tell me about "Faking It: Artificial Intelligence in a Human World".
CHATGPT: "Faking It: Artificial Intelligence in a Human World" is a book authored by Janelle Shane, published in 2019. In this book, Shane explores various aspects of artificial intelligence (AI) and its interactions with human society in a witty and accessible manner.

Shane delves into the world of AI by examining its successes, failures, and peculiarities. She discusses real-world applications of AI, ranging from self-driving cars and facial recognition systems to more whimsical uses such as generating art or writing poetry. Throughout the book, Shane uses humor and anecdotes to illustrate the complexities and limitations of AI technology.

One of the central themes of "Faking It" is the idea that AI systems often reflect the biases and limitations of their human creators. Shane highlights instances where AI algorithms have produced unexpected or unintended results due to biased training data or flawed programming. She also addresses ethical concerns surrounding AI, including issues related to privacy, fairness, and accountability.

Overall, "Faking It" offers an engaging and thought-provoking exploration of AI and its impact on society, inviting readers to consider the opportunities and challenges posed by this rapidly evolving technology.

This is again bullshit. I should know. I wrote *Faking It*, a book that was published in 2023, not in 2019. And my book doesn't talk about facial recognition, and barely mentions self-driving cars. Generative AI and the artificiality of artificial intelligence, rather than biased and flawed programming, are the central themes of my book.

To muddy the waters, ChatGPT wasn't completely wrong in its answer. Janelle Shane has indeed written a book about AI. But the title of her book is *You Look Like a Thing and I Love You: How Artificial Intelligence Works and Why It's Making the World a Weirder Place*. And her book was indeed published in 2019, and it talks at length about facial recognition and self-driving cars, with humour and anecdotes. This highlights how ChatGPT's hallucinations are often very plausible. However, plausible bullshit is the worst type of bullshit because people are more likely to believe it.

I queried ChatGPT about the author of *Faking It* several more times and each time it gave me a different answer. Julian Baggini, a philosopher of the mind, was next. Then Jaron Lanier, a pioneer of virtual reality. And finally, the roboticist Rodney Brooks. All plausible answers. But all wrong. In its aim to please, ChatGPT will always give you an answer, whether or not it is confident. With any large language model, there are probabilities behind the scenes. But OpenAI chose not to surface those probabilities. It could have said, "This is an answer I'm not confident about", "I'm highly certain about this", or even, "I can't answer this with any confidence". The best description I've heard is that ChatGPT is the perfect mansplainer.

The fact that ChatGPT hallucinates was no surprise. Two weeks before the release of ChatGPT, Meta (the company formerly known as Facebook) had itself released a large language model called Galactica, claiming that it would be the next interface for humans to access scientific knowledge. To this end, Galactica was trained on a "high-quality and highly curated corpus of humanity's scientific knowledge". The corpus included over 48 million scientific papers, scientific textbooks and encyclopedias, as well as descriptions of millions of compounds and proteins.

Yann LeCun, the chief AI scientist at Meta, predicted that Galactica would help scientists "summarize academic literature, solve math problems, generate Wiki articles, write scientific code, annotate molecules and proteins, and more". He even suggested that Galactica could "generate a scientific paper with references, formulas and everything". It quickly became clear, however, that Galactica would make science up, sometimes dangerous science. It produced, for example, a Wiki entry on the benefits of suicide, and another on the benefits of being white. It also wrote a research paper on the benefits of eating crushed glass.

After three days of criticism, Meta took Galactica down. LeCun responded aggressively on Twitter/X that the language model was being used for tasks it wasn't designed to do. This was despite the fact that Galactica's critics were trying to do the very things LeCun had suggested it could be used for, such as writing Wikis. Hallucination was thus a well-known problem with large language models before ChatGPT was released.

It was therefore a rather bold move for OpenAI to launch ChatGPT, knowing full well that it would frequently make things up. Sam Altman argued that "the world needs to get used to this. We need to make decisions together." And it became the mantra of OpenAI that it should get its products into the hands of the public, despite their flaws, and iterate fast to deal with any problems.

Unfortunately, hallucination isn't a problem that is going to go away. Indeed, it's not something you want to disappear completely. The only reason that ChatGPT can write a sonnet about falling in love with your laptop in the style of Shakespeare is because it can "hallucinate". Similarly the only way that ChatGPT can summarise a new court ruling is because it can say novel things. These are useful skills to have. The fundamental problem remains that large language models like ChatGPT don't know what is true, just what is probable. And we don't yet know how to do better than this.

What I take from the success of ChatGPT is that we've overestimated not machine intelligence but human intelligence. A lot of human communication is quite formulaic. We don't engage our brains as often as we think we do. Much of what we say is formulaic. And these formulas have now been taught to computers.

IDEA #4: ARTIFICIAL BRAINS

ELIZA

ChatGPT wasn't the first chatbot in the history of AI to catch the public's attention. That honour fell upon the very first chatbot, a system called ELIZA. This was written by Joseph Weizenbaum at MIT between 1964 and 1966. Weizenbaum had fled Nazi Germany as a young boy, and worked as a metrologist for the US Army during the Second World War, before ending up as a professor at MIT.

ELIZA was intended to be a computerised psychotherapist. In building ELIZA, Weizenbaum was interested in exploring the implications of AI. He didn't set out to deceive the public with ELIZA; indeed, his goals were quite the opposite. He wanted to demonstrate the superficiality of much of the communication between humans, even in sophisticated settings such as the therapist's office. To Weizenbaum's surprise and distress, many people using ELIZA thought they were conversing with a human.

ELIZA was named after the Cockney flower-girl Eliza Doolittle in George Bernard Shaw's play *Pygmalion* (later the musical *My Fair Lady*). The character Eliza could fool people with her high-class speech, but underneath she remained a working-class girl. Similarly, ELIZA could fool people into believing that it was far more than it was, and that it understood what people said.

ELIZA essentially exploited a party trick. It simply turned around what anyone said into a question. Given an input, "I've been thinking about my mortality," ELIZA inverted it into a question: "Why have you been thinking about your mortality?" Despite this simplicity, ELIZA produced some convincing dialogue. Indeed, Weizenbaum's secretary famously asked to be left alone with the computer terminal so she could talk to ELIZA in private.

Here's a sample dialogue:

> **ELIZA**: Please tell me what's been bothering you.
> **ME**: Oh, hello, ELIZA. It's been a long time.
> **ELIZA**: Hi. What seems to be your problem?
> **ME**: Lately, I've been feeling a little depressed.
> **ELIZA**: And how do you feel right now?
> **ME**: I feel sad, but relieved to be writing.
> **ELIZA**: Of what does feeling sad remind you?
> **ME**: Well, I'm an alcoholic, and I've been sober for a long time, but I drank yesterday. And then I decided to stop drinking again. But still; that makes me feel sad.
> **ELIZA**: Is it because you are an alcoholic that you came to me?
> **ME**: I suppose that that's one of the reasons.
> **ELIZA**: Can you elaborate on that?
> **ME**: I mean, it's not the only reason, but alcoholism is a primary thing that has messed up my life.

ELIZA was intended to be a "parody" of a psychotherapist. Weizenbaum was therefore shocked that several psychiatrists proposed ELIZA be used as a clinical tool. Indeed, if he were alive today, Weizenbaum would likely be upset that this has now become reality. In Germany, an AI chatbot not that much more capable than ELIZA is helping many asylum seekers deal with their post-traumatic stress disorder. Having fled war zones or having had terrible experiences crossing into Europe,

PTSD is common among asylum seekers. And sadly there are too few human therapists available to help them all, so an AI chatbot is being used instead. It's not ideal. But perhaps it's better than nothing?

SCALING LAWS

OpenAI has bet hundreds of millions of dollars on scaling the GPT family of models ever larger. This wasn't actually as risky as it sounds, due to some remarkable scaling laws. These aren't fundamental laws like Newton's laws of motion. They don't reflect, as far as we know, the physics of the universe. These scaling laws are empirical: they reflect observational findings about how more parameters, more computation and more training data lead to improvements in the performance of neural networks.

These laws suggest that the performance of systems in the GPT family scales vary consistently with increasing model size

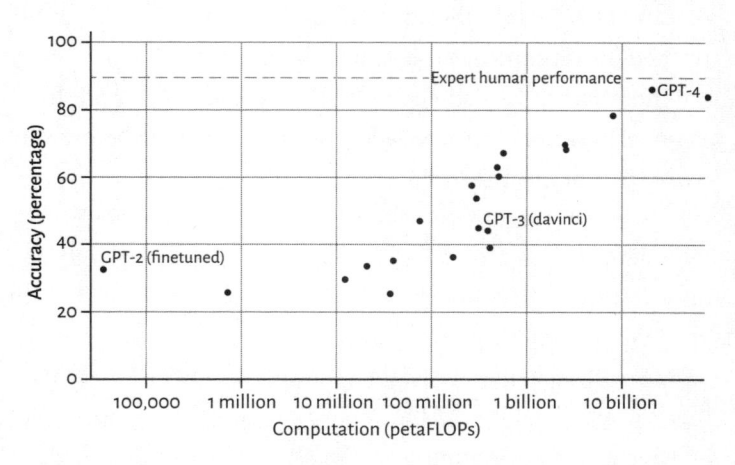

Performance of large language models on a standard multiple-choice knowledge test against the amount of computation used to train models.

(measured by the number of parameters), increasing training (measured by the number of computer cycles) and increasing training data (measured by the number of tokens in the training set). Indeed, it appears that simple mathematical relationships (so-called power laws) tie together these four measures.

This means that we can very accurately predict performance as we scale systems. In simple terms, if we increase the computation budget tenfold, the number of parameters in the model and the number of tokens for training the model should also scale approximately tenfold.

But here we run into a fundamental problem. We cannot simply increase computation and training data tenfold repeatedly. GPUs are now in short supply as companies, and even nations, compete for access to the computational infrastructure to build ever larger models. And we're running out of data, or at least high-quality data. For example, GPT-3 was trained on a significant fraction of the internet.

There has to be something else we can do? After all, humans managed to learn to walk, talk, read and write before we had access to the internet ...

IDEA #5:

REWARDING SUCCESS

THIS BRINGS US TO reinforcement learning, the fifth and penultimate idea in this history of artificial intelligence. It's an idea that is again stolen from nature: ***You can learn from experience, rewarding success and penalising failure.***

We learn many things by trying them out. We get on a bicycle. We fall off. We get back on. We ride a little longer. We fall off. Slowly but surely, we learn to do more of the right things, and avoid more of the wrong things. Perhaps computers can learn in a similar way?

This idea is more complex than it first sounds. Consider learning to play chess. Suppose you play a game and lose. You need to penalise this failure, so you don't make the same mistakes again. But which were the moves that led to failure? Even when you lose, many moves might have been good moves. Perhaps it just wasn't possible to compensate for a mistake made early on. How, then, do you identify the bad moves?

On the other hand, suppose that you win the game. You need now to reward this success. But which moves led to success? Even when you win, there might be any number of poor moves you made that were not bad enough to lose the game. Equally there might have been one killer move that won the match. This is a famous problem in AI. It is called the "credit assignment" problem. Where do we assign credit, given that we only get a signal of win or lose at the end of the game? It's the problem of distributing the credit for winning and the blame for losing across the many different moves made in playing a game.

One of the earliest AI researchers, Donald Michie, used reinforcement learning to play noughts and crosses with a matchbox computer. A colleague at Edinburgh University had bet Michie that he could not build a learning machine. Indeed, Michie's colleague argued that such a machine was impossible. So, in 1960, Michie built MENACE, the **M**achine **E**ducable **N**oughts **a**nd **C**rosses **E**ngine, to prove him wrong. MENACE was a computer built out of matchboxes which used reinforcement learning to play noughts and crosses. In fact, MENACE learnt to play noughts and crosses perfectly. It was impossible to beat.

Mitchie's matchbox computer was simple. It was made from 304 matchboxes. Each matchbox represented a different possible layout of a noughts and crosses grid. It turns out that there are 304 unique arrangements of the grid, ignoring rotations and mirror images. MENACE started each game playing noughts. (To get MENACE to play second would simply require more matchboxes.) Each square on the noughts and crosses grid had a different colour. And the matchboxes contained marbles of these nine different colours. A marble would first be removed at random from the matchbox representing the

IDEA #5: REWARDING SUCCESS

A recreation of the MENACE matchbox computer built in 2015 by Matthew Scroggs.

current state of the grid. The colour of the marble would then determine where MENACE placed its next nought.

At the end of the game, if MENACE had won, the coloured marbles were returned to their respective matchboxes, along with three bonus marbles of the same colour to reward the successful play. On the other hand, if MENACE had lost, no marbles were returned at all, penalising the moves leading to the loss. Credit assignment in MENACE was thus rather simple. All moves in a winning game were rewarded, and all moves in a losing game were penalised. This straightforward assignment of credit is good enough to learn to play a simple game like noughts and crosses. After a few hundred games, MENACE played noughts and crosses perfectly. If MENACE's opponent made a mistake, MENACE would win. And otherwise, MENACE would always draw. MENACE could not be beaten. Take that, humanity – beaten by a collection of inanimate matchboxes!

Games like chess or noughts and crosses are obvious domains in which to apply reinforcement learning, because there's a clear measure of success. Did you win? And you can learn through self-play – that is, having the computer play against itself. But reinforcement learning can also be applied to teach robots to do tasks like walking or picking up objects.

Michie later used his reinforcement learning method to teach a robot to balance a pole. However, such robot learning is much slower than playing a game in a virtual world. And when robot learning goes wrong, you might have broken the robot. Indeed, for these reasons, robots are increasingly being trained by using reinforcement learning not in the real world but in simulation.

Michie's interest in AI went back to the very beginning of the field. Prior to working at Edinburgh, he was a codebreaker at Bletchley Park. There he befriended Alan Turing, with the two bonding over meals together and a shared inability to play chess well. This itself led to Michie and Turing wondering whether machines could be taught to play chess, and, grander still, whether machines could think.

I met Michie many years after he had built MENACE, and he told me several amusing anecdotes about Turing's time codebreaking at Bletchley Park. For example, fearful of a German invasion, Turing buried a number of silver bars in the grounds of the country house. But Turing failed to record the location of these bars. The silver therefore remains buried to this day. And while at Bletchley, Turing was also precious about his tea mug, chaining it to the radiator in Hut 8. But the radiator was too far from the sink for the mug to ever be washed. As a result, many people – Mitchie included – feared for Turing's health.

IDEA #5: REWARDING SUCCESS

DEEPMIND

We now come to AI's next breakout moment. This came from the company DeepMind, founded in 2010 by Demis Hassabis and Shane Legg, two AI researchers from University College London, as well as Mustafa Suleyman, a social activist and childhood friend of Demis Hassabis's younger brother.

Demis Hassabis (left) and Mustafa Suleyman.

Since its founding, DeepMind has had an outsized influence on the field of AI. Of its three founders, Legg has kept a low profile (which I respect by not picturing him here) but Hassabis and Suleyman have not. Demis Hassabis – or Sir Demis Hassabis, to give him his full title – currently leads the AI efforts at Google, while Mustafa Suleyman leads the rival AI efforts at Microsoft. I suspect it should be better known that a big part of AI's future thus rests in the hands of two friends who first met at a boys' grammar school in North London.

Hassabis was a child prodigy, learning to play chess at age four, reaching master level at just 13 years old, and captaining several English junior teams. In his gap year, before going up to study at Cambridge University, Hassabis worked as a game designer. His 1994 game *Theme Park* sold millions of copies and paid his way through university. Hassabis then got a double first in computer science from Cambridge, followed by a PhD in cognitive neuroscience from University College London. With thick glasses and boyish looks, Hassabis reminds me of Brains, the scientific genius and engineer in the *Thunderbirds* TV series.

Mustafa Suleyman, on the other hand, came from a less technical background than Hassabis or Legg. He went up to Oxford University to study philosophy and theology, but quickly dropped out to have a more practical impact on the world. He helped start the Muslim Youth Helpline, which would become one of the largest mental health support services for Muslims in the United Kingdom. Mustafa then worked for Ken Livingstone, the mayor of London, on human rights issues, before tackling social problems for the United Nations, the Dutch government and the World Wide Fund for Nature.

Shane Legg is from Rotorua, New Zealand. He got an undergraduate degree in computing and mathematical sciences from the University of Waikato, and a master's degree in mathematics from the University of Auckland. He then worked at several software companies, including the AGI start-up Webmind. He wrote a PhD on machine super intelligence at the Dalle Molle Institute for Artificial Intelligence in Switzerland, then landed a postdoctoral position at University College London in the Gatsby Computational Neuroscience Unit, where he met Demis Hassabis.

In 2010, the three teamed up to found DeepMind. The

company has an ambitious but uncomplicated mission: to solve artificial intelligence, and then use that artificial intelligence to solve humanity's problems. DeepMind started this mission by learning to play games using reinforcement learning. It began with 49 different Atari video games, including such classics as *Pong*, *Breakout* and *Space Invaders*.

The results stunned the AI research community. DeepMind's AI program was not given any background knowledge about the games. It just had access to the score and the raw pixels on the screen. Yet it somehow managed to learn to play each game well from first principles. In most cases, DeepMind's AI was able to play at the level of a human. And in a dozen cases, it played at superhuman level.

Unlike a human coming to these games, DeepMind's AI didn't know about bats, balls or walls. Nor did it know about momentum, gravity or any of the other things that help us play such games. DeepMind's AI learnt every game from scratch. By playing itself lots and lots of times, the computer learnt first how to play, and then, after a few more hours of training, how to play well.

Stuart Russell, a leading AI researcher and author of the most popular textbook on AI, captured the mood of many of us working in the field: "That's both impressive and scary in the sense that if a human baby was born and by the evening of its first day was already beating human beings at video games, you'd be terrified." Realising the potential, Google quickly paid what is rumoured to be around half a billion dollars to acquire DeepMind. The company had no paying customers and just 50 employees.

ALL SYSTEMS GO

DeepMind's next breakthrough came half a dozen years later, capturing headlines across the world. It has been described as AI's Sputnik moment.

In October 1957, the world's first artificial satellite, Sputnik, was lifted into low Earth orbit from the Baikonur Cosmodrome in Kazakhstan. Sputnik wasn't much to look at, a polished metal sphere about the size of a large pumpkin. And all it could do was broadcast radio pulses from its four external antennas. But Sputnik (like DeepMind's next breakthrough) changed the world. It woke the United States up to the threat of Russia's technical advances and started the Space Race. This technological race would take man to the Moon, rovers to Mars and spacecraft to every planet in the Solar System. And it would give to humanity everything from intercontinental ballistic missiles to integrated circuits.

AI's Sputnik moment occurred nearly 60 years later, in March 2016, with the victory of DeepMind's AI program AlphaGo against a human. The program wasn't playing against just any human, but rather one of the world's best players of the ancient Chinese game of Go. AlphaGo's victory was, according to many observers, the event that started the AI race. This time it wasn't the United States that awoke to a potential technological threat but China. And it wasn't a race to the Moon, but a race for dominance in the next great economic revolution.

Shortly after this AI victory, the Chinese government announced an ambitious plan to lead the world in AI. The Chinese plan estimates that, by 2030, AI will contribute over

US$150 billion directly to China's industrial output, and over US$1.5 trillion indirectly via related industries.

How could a computer winning a simple boardgame have such an impact on China's long-term ambitions? It's important to understand that Go has a special importance in China. The game was invented there over 2000 years ago. It is one of the four cultivated arts of a scholar gentleman, along with calligraphy, painting and playing the musical instrument guqin. Go is a game of immense subtlety and complexity. Indeed, AlphaGo's victory was sufficiently disturbing that the Chinese authorities banned live-streaming of AlphaGo's games.

China's AI plan does little to hide China's ambition to use artificial intelligence to gain economic and military dominance over the world. As the Chinese president, Xi Jinping, reported to the 19th Party Congress in October 2017, China aims to become the "science and technology superpower" of the coming century. And they've been executing this plan. China is, for example, now neck and neck with the United States in terms of AI publications and patents.

Many other countries have responded to the Chinese AI plan. Not surprisingly, the United States has a plan to counter the threat of China winning the AI race, and has announced billions of dollars in federal funding to back this up. The United Kingdom, another major player in AI research, looks to spend several billion pounds to keep the UK in this race. France's plan to participate in the AI race will cost 1.5 billion euros. Germany plans to spend 3 billion euros. Even India is looking to invest around US$0.5 billion in AI. Sadly, the Australian government still has made only modest investments in this area, and thus looks set to miss out.

There is little doubt that artificial intelligence is transforming the current economic, political and societal landscape. A study by PwC in 2017 estimated that global GDP could be around 15 per cent higher in 2030 as a result of AI. This is equivalent to an additional US$15 trillion in inflation-adjusted terms. This would make it one of the largest opportunities for innovation in the next decade.

AlphaGo's victory represented an important step on that path to AI innovation. Many Go masters had predicted computers would never play Go well. Even AI optimists had predicted success was still a decade or more away. In July 1997, following IBM Deep Blue's victory against Garry Kasparov at the game of chess, the *New York Times* had said, "When or if a computer defeats a human Go champion, it will be a sign that artificial intelligence is truly beginning to become as good as the real thing."

The *New York Times* had a point. Go is a significantly harder, more complex problem than chess. In chess, there are about 20 possible moves to consider at each turn. In Go, there are around 200. Looking two steps forwards, there are 200 times 200 – 40,000 – possible moves to consider. Three steps forwards, there are 8 million different moves to consider. And looking just 15 black-and-white stones ahead requires considering more possible moves than there are atoms in the universe.

Another aspect of Go that makes it immensely challenging is working out who is winning. In chess, it's not too hard to work out who is ahead. Just counting the value of the different captured pieces is a good first approximation. In Go, counting surrounded stones doesn't give you a clear idea, as surrounded stones can themselves easily be surrounded. It takes Go masters a lifetime of training to learn who is ahead. And any good Go program needs to work out who is ahead when deciding which of those 200 different moves to make.

To recognise who is ahead, AlphaGo used reinforcement learning. We don't really know how to describe a good position on the Go board. But just like humans can learn to perceive good positions, a computer can learn too. Google's engineering expertise and vast server farms also played a significant role in the victory. AlphaGo played itself billions of times, improving its strategies. Indeed, AlphaGo played more games of Go than a human could in a lifetime of playing the game. Like a lot of recent advances in AI, a significant return has come from throwing a ridiculous amount of resources at the problem.

MOVE 37

One move in the 2016 match between Go master Lee Sedol and AlphaGo was pivotal: move 37 in the second game. By one of those amazing coincidences that is too improbable to make up, it was also move 37 in the second game of the famous 1997 match between Garry Kasparov and IBM's Deep Blue that proved pivotal.

In the 1997 match, Kasparov had won the first game. Deep Blue began the second game with a Spanish opening. This is one of the most popular openings in chess, played by beginners and experts alike. At the 37th move, Deep Blue broke with chess convention by forgoing a simple material gain for a narrow positional advantage. Kasparov resigned shortly afterwards.

Kasparov was livid, claiming that IBM must be cheating. He argued that only a human could have come up with such a subtle but good move. He demanded that IBM provide computer logs to prove that Deep Blue had come up with the move, and not one of the human experts working with IBM. IBM declined to do so. Later analysis suggested that it might have been a bug – as Deep Blue was running out of time, the program had simply chosen to make a rather random move. Indeed, Kasparov didn't need to resign this game, as a draw was possible by perpetual check. But Kasparov was spooked.

Kasparov deep in thought against Deep Blue in 1997.

In the 2016 match between Lee Sedol and AlphaGo, the first game had been won by AlphaGo. Lee was therefore keen to get back into the match. And at move 37 of game two, AlphaGo made a move that no expert human would. It played on the fifth line of the board. Conventional wisdom from thousands of years of human play is that you play on the fourth line – not the fifth – at such an early point of the game.

Lee, like Kasparov nearly two decades earlier, was visibly rattled. He left the tournament room and took nearly 15 minutes to return and continue the game. Move 37 had again turned the course of the game and played a crucial role in the outcome of the match. Lee lost this second game, and eventually lost the match 4–1. Afterwards Lee described AlphaGo's move as "beautiful".

Unlike in 1997, move 37 wasn't a bug this time. In fact, move 37 was a nearly perfect move, found by a computer able to consider many more possibilities than a human mind could. Go experts are excited. They expect their game to be transformed by AI-powered insights such as this. Just as chess has been enhanced by computer programs that play much better chess than humans, Go will likely be revolutionised by computer programs that play much better Go than humans.

It's worth remembering that AI didn't take the fun out of playing chess for humans. No chess master can beat a good computer program today. But more people now earn a living playing chess professionally than back in 1997. And the standard of both the professional and the amateur game has increased significantly. Amateurs can now practise against skilled opponents who are infinitely patient. And experts can now easily study and understand new and subtle lines of play.

If there's one history lesson we can take from these two stories about move 37, it is that AI will surprise humans with *how* it beats us.

FOLDING PROTEINS

DeepMind has, of course, grander ambitions than just playing games better than humans. Ultimately it wants to "solve AI", and then solve humanity's problems using AI. And what better place to start than biology? Or, to be more precise, predicting protein structure, the three-dimensional shape of a protein based on its amino acid sequence. Protein structure prediction was one of the most important open problems in biology, challenging biologists for over 50 years.

Proteins are large biological molecules that help keep us alive. They carry oxygen to our muscles, catalyse metabolic reactions, help transmit nerve signals and play a vital role in photosynthesis and many other biological reactions. To understand how proteins do all these amazing things, you need to understand their shape. Shape determines function. All of us are, for example, far too aware of the important role the spike protein plays in the ability of the SARS-CoV-2 virus to infect us.

In 1958, John Kendrew was the first scientist to identify the structure of a protein, myoglobin. He shared the 1962 Nobel Prize in Chemistry for this discovery. Since then, the structures of about 170,000 other proteins have been discovered. There are, however, over 200 million proteins found in biology. And uncovering the structure of a new protein might take several years of effort and be worthy of a PhD.

Protein structure prediction was a good choice of problem for DeepMind to tackle, as biologists had turned it into a game. Every two years, there's a "world championship" in protein structure prediction. Around 100 research groups from around the world participate regularly. And competition is tough. Researchers spend years preparing computer programs to predict protein structure.

Before 2018, computational methods had limited accuracy compared to experimental techniques, except on small and simple proteins. Then DeepMind entered an AI program called AlphaFold into the competition for the first time. It won, beating 97 other entrants. AlphaFold predicted the most accurate structure for 25 out of 43 proteins, compared with just three out of 43 for the second-placed team. Two years later, in 2020, DeepMind did even better. Its new transformer-based model again won the competition, with its results described by biologists as "astounding" and "transformational". AlphaFold determined the shape of around two-thirds of the proteins, with accuracy comparable to laboratory experiments.

Reinforcement learning plays an important role in AlphaFold. It is used iteratively to refine the predicted protein shape by learning from previous prediction errors. The model is rewarded based on how closely its predicted structures match the known or experimentally determined structures, effectively guiding it towards more accurate predictions. This iterative process helps the model explore a vast space of potential shapes, learning to balance the exploration of new folded shapes and the exploitation of known structural information.

In 2022, DeepMind did not enter the competition. There was no need, as, having open-sourced AlphaFold, most of the entrants now used AlphaFold or tools incorporating AlphaFold. DeepMind instead turned its energies to using AlphaFold to predict the structure of proteins. In July 2023, it released a database with the structure of 200 million proteins for scientists to use freely. This database includes nearly every protein known to science. Janet Thornton, director emeritus of the European Bioinformatics Institute, which hosts the database, described its impact well: "Scientists build on the shoulders of giants. Most often, those shoulders are data. Having these millions of structure predictions will change the face of biology. This is useful for medicine, agriculture, biotech, everything – it's just fantastic."[1]

ELEMENTARY, DEAR WATSON

As we've seen, DeepMind isn't the only company that has beaten humanity at one of its own games: IBM also did so in 1997 with the game of chess. IBM's Deep Blue project easily paid for itself. The day after Deep Blue's victory against Garry Kasparov, IBM's shares jumped nearly 4 per cent, adding around US$2 billion to the value of the company. The chess victory also created a lot of favourable publicity for IBM as a technology leader. Unsurprisingly, IBM was keen to repeat this success with an even more challenging game.

In 2007, a team at IBM led by David Ferrucci started developing Watson, an AI program to play *Jeopardy!*, a popular general knowledge game. Watson was named after IBM's founder and first CEO, Thomas J. Watson. And at over 40 seasons long, *Jeopardy!* is one of the longest-running and most popular quiz shows on TV. Rather than being given questions, contestants in *Jeopardy!* are given clues in the form of answers. They must identify the person, place, thing or idea that the clue describes, phrasing each response in the form of a question.

> **QUESTION**: Born in Germany, he began composing in England in 1710 and decomposing in Westminster Abbey in 1759.
> **ANSWER**: Who is George Frideric Handel?

Before you complain that you can just Google the answer, Watson wasn't connected to the internet. It did, however, have access to 4 terabytes of information extracted from encyclopedias, dictionaries, thesauruses, news articles and literary works. Watson was a collection of lots of different AI programs. There was, for example, one AI program that was an expert at answering geography questions, one for historical events and another for taxonomies. *Jeopardy!* contestants have to bet on certain questions, so Watson used reinforcement learning to come up with a good betting strategy. It also had a mechanical "hand" to buzz into questions, just like the human contestants.

After four years of development, Watson was ready to take on humans. In early 2011, a match was arranged against *Jeopardy!* champions Ken Jennings and Brad Rutter. Rutter is the highest-earning American game show contestant ever, having won over US$5 million in prizes on various game shows. He also holds the record for the longest winning streak on *Jeopardy!*, with 74 consecutive wins. Jennings is the second-highest-earning American game show contestant ever. He had never lost a match in any appearance on *Jeopardy!* This was about to change.

Over the two-day competition against Jennings and Rutter, IBM's Watson was the clear victor, winning US$77,147. Jennings ended with US$24,000, while Rutter finished with just US$21,600. Man had again been beaten by machine. Watson took home the overall prize of US$1 million, which was donated to charity.

Ken Jennings, the AI Watson and Brad Rutter competing at *Jeopardy!* for a US$1 million prize.

All in all, IBM invested many millions of dollars and several years of effort to build Watson. The supercomputer on which Watson ran itself cost around US$3 million. Today, however, ChatGPT can compete for free with a simple prompt. I gave it a go:

IDEA #5: REWARDING SUCCESS

ME: They're the two states you could be re-entering if you're crossing Florida's northern border. Answer in the form of a question as on the quiz show *Jeopardy!*
CHATGPT: What are Georgia and Alabama?
ME: Invented in the 1500s to speed up the game, this manoeuvre involves two pieces of the same colour.
CHATGPT: What is castling in chess?
ME: Though it sounds "harsh", it's just embroidery, often in a floral pattern, done with yarn on cotton cloth.
CHATGPT: What is crewel work?
ME: He was presidentially pardoned on September 8, 1974.
CHATGPT: Who is Richard Nixon?
ME: In 1594 he took a job as a tax collector in Andalusia.
CHATGPT: Who is Miguel de Cervantes?
ME: Its largest airport is named for a World War II hero; its second largest, for a World War II battle.
CHATGPT: What is Chicago?

The last question is particularly historic: it was the final question in Watson's 2011 match against Jennings and Rutter. Watson guessed Toronto, despite the question category being US cities. While ChatGPT answered correctly, this is not a real test as this question (and the answer) are undoubtably now in ChatGPT's training data.

Analysis of Watson's performance in the match against Jennings and Rutter identified that Watson wasn't better than the human champions at answering questions. It was just better at gambling. It could more accurately calculate the probability it had the correct answer and bet accordingly. This ability of computers to better calculate probabilities neatly takes us to the sixth and final idea explaining the progress we've made towards building AI. We'll explore this idea in the next chapter.

HUMAN FEEDBACK

I end with one final success of reinforcement learning. This concerns ChatGPT. You will recall that, to build the GPT family of large language models, OpenAI took Google's transformer model and scaled it aggressively. But to get from GPT-3 to ChatGPT, they added one important new ingredient: reinforcement learning from human feedback (often shortened to RLHF).

Large language models like GPT-2 and GPT-3 can behave as if they have attention deficit disorder. You will recall that these models are random, producing different output each time they are run. And the problem with randomness is that the dice eventually go against you. Mathematicians call it gambler's ruin. With models like GPT-2 and GPT-3, this manifests itself in a model that is easily distracted. These models write sentences by repeatedly predicting the next word. Eventually, however, a word is predicted that takes the output off in a random and unwanted direction. Let me give you a simple example. I asked GPT-2 to continue "Photosynthesis is". It started well:

> **PHOTOSYNTHESIS IS** the process by which living things grow and produce their own energy ...

IDEA #5: REWARDING SUCCESS

But then it started to go wrong:

... and carbon dioxide (CO$_2$).

Photosynthesis produces oxygen, not carbon dioxide. GPT2 made more errors in the next sentence:

Most plants and animal photosynthesize carbon in one of two ways.

This is grammatically wrong – it should be "animals", not "animal". But even more critically, animals don't perform photosynthesis (though a few form symbiotic relationships with algae and cyanobacteria that do).

Reinforcement learning from human feedback tackles this problem. There's a training phase in which humans are repeatedly asked which of two possible outputs of the large language model they prefer. Human feedback ensures that appropriate values are incorporated into the model. If humans down-rank racist and sexist answers, then the model learns to output better answers.

Since it involves humans, reinforcement learning from human feedback is an expensive process. But it improves the output of large language models dramatically. It ensures that large language models, most of which have been trained rather indiscriminately on internet data, don't repeat the misinformation, propaganda, conspiracy theories, racism and sexism found online. On top of this, the developers of large language models hand-code some explicit guardrails into the system to try to filter out some of the more offensive, dangerous and illegal content that they produce.

All in all, it's pretty amazing how well large language models can be made to write using reinforcement learning, considering the poor quality of a lot of the data on which they're trained!

IDEA #6:

REASONING ABOUT BELIEFS

WE COME NOW TO THE sixth and final idea used in building AI systems. The world is uncertain; AI systems therefore need to deal with uncertainty when interacting with the world. How certain is the autonomous car that it is safe to overtake at this moment? What probability does the computer vision algorithm give to this X-ray being clear of cancer? How likely is it that this incoming email is spam?

Fortunately, 250 years ago the Reverend Thomas Bayes, a Presbyterian minister from Tunbridge Wells in Kent, proposed a principled way to deal with uncertainty. In particular, he derived a theorem that provides an elegant way for computers to calculate probabilities. A simple example will illustrate the power of Bayes' theorem.

The example is a little technical, but I assure you, it's worth it. And you're good for it. You're coming to the end of this brief history of AI, so you're practically an expert in AI now. Just think – in two pages' time, you'll be able to boast that you derived Bayes' theorem for yourself. From first principles! So stay with me.

Suppose you're building a Covid detector based on how people cough. You decide to train a neural network to do this. You've read a few books on AI so you use a transformer model to recognise the sort of bad cough associated with Covid. It seems to work well. But can you be sure? Bayes' theorem can help. You want to compute the accuracy of your Covid detector. That is, you want to compute the probability that a person has Covid (your hypothesis), given that your detector registers that they have a suspicious cough (your evidence). In symbols:

prob(has Covid | suspicious cough)

This is the "prob"ability that a person "has Covid" given that (the vertical bar, " | ") they have a "suspicious cough".

It's not easy to compute this conditional probability directly. You'd have to give the detector thousands of audio files, then check clinically that the dozens of people that the detector flags with suspicious coughs do indeed have Covid. And every time you update the detector, you'd have to compute this painfully again by hand.

The Reverend Bayes fortunately gave us a better way. There are three other related probabilities you can compute more easily which allow you to compute the accuracy of the detector. First, you invert the conditional probability, and compute the probability that people with Covid are correctly identified by your detector as having a suspicious cough. That is:

prob(suspicious cough | has Covid)

IDEA #6: REASONING ABOUT BELIEFS

This sounds similar but is, in fact, much easier to calculate. You need to consider only the much smaller pool of people with Covid. You get them to use your detector, and simply count which fraction are flagged as suspicious. Suppose 95 per cent of people with Covid are correctly flagged as having a suspicious cough. Then *prob(suspicious cough | has Covid)* = 0.95.

Second, you compute the probability of the hypothesis. That is, you compute the probability that a person in the wider population has Covid. This is again easy to do, given some historical data. It doesn't depend on your detector, so you don't need to recompute it each time you update the detector. You can, for example, compute it indirectly by analysing wastewater. In symbols, we write this probability as:

prob(has Covid)

Let's suppose that 2 per cent of the population currently have Covid. That is *prob(has Covid)* = 0.02.

Third, you compute the probability of the evidence. That is, you compute the probability that a person is flagged by your detector as having a suspicious cough. This can simply be done by giving your detector thousands of audio files and counting which fraction are flagged as suspicious. You don't need to care about whether they actually have Covid or not. In symbols, we write this probability as:

prob(suspicious cough)

Alternatively, if you know the false positive rate of the detector (the fraction of people without Covid who are flagged as having a suspicious cough), you don't even need to measure this; you can compute it directly.

Suppose the false positive rate is 5 per cent. That is, 5 per cent of people without Covid are incorrectly identified by the detector as having a suspicious cough. You can break the calculation of the probability that a person is flagged as having a suspicious cough, *prob(suspicious cough)*, into two parts. First, we know that 2 per cent of the people sampled have Covid, and the detector correctly identifies 95 per cent of them as having a suspicious cough. Second, the other 98 per cent of the population don't have Covid. The detector incorrectly identifies 5 per cent of them with a suspicious cough. Hence, the fraction of people flagged correctly or incorrectly with a suspicious cough is (0.02 × 0.95) + (0.98 × 0.05), or 0.068. That is, 6.8 per cent of people are flagged by the detector as having a suspicious cough. So *prob(suspicious cough)* = 0.068.

We can now use these three probabilities to calculate the detector accuracy. This is thanks to a beautiful relationship between these four probabilities that Bayes himself identified. It's such a simple idea that we can derive it formally here from first principles.

Suppose we try our detector out on 1000 people. Since 2 per cent of the population have Covid (recall *prob(has Covid)* = 0.02), 20 of these 1000 people will have Covid. We also know that the detector is not perfect and only 95 per cent of these 20 people with Covid will actually be flagged as having a suspicious cough (recall *prob(suspicious cough | has Covid)* = 0.95).

95 per cent of 20 is 19. Thus our detector will flag 19 out of these 20 people with Covid as having a suspicious cough.

We also know that 6.8 per cent of people are flagged by the detector as having a suspicious cough (recall *prob(suspicious cough)* = 0.068). Therefore, of the 1000 people tested, 68 will be flagged as having a suspicious cough. But we just calculated that only 19 of the people flagged with a suspicious cough *actually* has Covid. Hence the fraction of people with a suspicious cough that has Covid is 19/68 or 0.279. That is, just 27.9 per cent of people flagged by the detector with a suspicious cough actually have Covid.

In fact, the 1000 people were irrelevant – we'd get the same answer with 10,000 or even 100,000 people. Bayes' theorem codifies this reasoning, telling us that these four probabilities are related by a simple and beautiful equation:

$$\text{prob(has Covid | suspicious cough)}$$
$$= \frac{\text{prob(suspicious cough | has Covid)} \times \text{prob(has Covid)}}{\text{prob(suspicious cough)}}$$
$$= \frac{0.95 \times 0.02}{0.068}$$
$$= 0.279$$

So while our detector correctly identifies 95 per cent of people with Covid as also having a suspicious cough, there's only a 27.9 per cent chance that a random person the detector flags with a suspicious cough actually has Covid. Put another way, most of the time, when the detector flags a person with a suspicious cough, that person doesn't actually have Covid. It seems our detector isn't very good after all!

The problem is that the majority of people don't have Covid. Therefore, testing people at random, even with a fairly accurate coughing test, is likely to throw up a lot of false positives. This reasoning isn't just important for interpreting the results of an AI Covid detector. It can be used in many other AI systems, from recognising speech to recommending movies. Indeed, Bayes' theorem is such an important building block that it is often considered to be "to the theory of probability what Pythagoras's theorem is to geometry".[1] And it has become an integral tool in calculating probabilities in many AI systems. The sixth idea central to AI today, therefore, is: ***You can compute the probability of an event, given evidence about the event, using Bayes' theorem.***

Bayes' theorem is used today in many different applications. It's the reason that you get much less spam email than you used to receive – your email filter uses Bayes' theorem to compute the probability that a new email is spam. The recommendation engine in Netflix also uses Bayes' theorem to compute the probability that you'll like a particular movie. And its predictions are pretty accurate – four out of five movies that people watch on Netflix are not movies that they logged in to watch but rather movies that the system recommends.[2] And, back in the 1970s, the US Navy used Bayes' theorem to compute the most probable paths of Soviet nuclear subs.

Sadly, we know very little about the mathematical mastermind behind this important idea. The Reverend Thomas Bayes was born in 1701 or 1702, possibly in Hertfordshire. He became a Presbyterian minister after studying logic and theology at the University of Edinburgh. He died in 1761, having only published two works, a treatise on divinity and a defence of Newton's calculus. His work on probability was published two years after his death by his friend, mathematician and fellow theologian the Reverend Richard Price. Price himself has been considered "the greatest Welsh thinker of all time", having contributed important ideas to theology, finance, economics, probability and life insurance.[3] Bayes may have been much less prolific, but his one idea about calculating probabilities makes him one of the most influential mathematicians to have ever lived.

WHERE AM I?

We come now to a chicken-or-egg problem – a wonderful example of the wide-ranging applications of Bayes' idea. It's an

The Reverend Thomas Bayes.

AI technique that goes by the name of simultaneous localisation and mapping – or, as everyone in the field calls it, SLAM.

Suppose you're Waymo and want to build a self-driving car. You put an expensive lidar sensor on top of the car. (Lidar is the light version of radar. A rotating laser light beam reflects off objects, and the time of flight is used to measure their distance away.) And you use the data from that and other sensors to do two things: to map the world, identifying where obstacles like pedestrians and cyclists are that can't be found on your GPS map, and to locate exactly where the car is in that changing world.

That's where you run into this particular chicken-or-egg problem. You can't locate yourself without an up-to-date map of the world. But you can't construct an up-to-date map of the world without locating yourself (and the sensor). We somehow need to do both simultaneously. And this chicken-or-egg problem is solved by SLAM. It uses Bayes' idea to simultaneously update the probable location of both the car and the objects in its map of the world.

In fact, it may be that AI researchers are unintentionally reproducing parts of the human brain. There is evidence that the hippocampus, the part of the human brain involved in spatial reasoning and memory, appears to be involved in SLAM-like computations.

Self-driving cars lean heavily on high-definition maps and GPS. But there's only so far you can go with GPS: maps are always out of date; GPS can be blocked by tunnels and urban canyons; and obstacles like pedestrians, cyclists and other cars aren't found on maps but need to be avoided.

IDEA #6: REASONING ABOUT BELIEFS

A self-driving car therefore needs to be able to map its own environment.

Stanley, the self-driving car that won the US$2 million DARPA challenge by driving across the Mojave Desert without a human driver in 2005, used SLAM to locate and map its environment, gathering data from a host of sensors: lidar, GPS, cameras and gyroscopes. Stanley could thereby generate high-precision 3D maps of the world that are accurate to within 4–5 centimetres.

Self-driving cars like Stanley will one day dramatically reduce the number of road fatalities, cut energy consumption, fit cars more densely onto crowded roads, free commuters for more productive (or more fun) activities and give mobility to those currently denied it like the young, the old and those with disabilities. Why, then, is it taking us so long to have full self-driving cars? The Society of Automotive Engineers has identified five levels of autonomy. Well, six, if you count none!

- **Level 0 (No Automation)**: A human controls everything, even if the car has features like automatic emergency braking.

- **Level 1 (Driver Assistance)**: The car can assist with either steering or acceleration/deceleration using information about the driving environment. However, a human is still responsible for most tasks.

- **Level 2 (Partial Automation)**: The car can control both steering and acceleration/deceleration but requires a human to remain engaged and monitor the driving environment at all times.

- **Level 3 (Conditional Automation):** The car can handle all aspects of driving in certain conditions, but a human must be ready to take over when the system requests.

- **Level 4 (High Automation):** The car can perform all driving tasks and monitor the driving environment, but only in certain conditions or environments. Human intervention is not needed in these specific scenarios, but it may be required in others.

- **Level 5 (Full Automation):** The car can perform all driving tasks, under all conditions without any human intervention.

Currently, the most advanced self-driving cars commercially available are somewhere between Level 3 and 4. For instance, the self-driving taxis being piloted in San Francisco and a few other US cities are at Level 4. However, getting to Level 5 – full automation – remains a major challenge, despite Elon Musk's many promises. We'll need to deal with many factors, including adverse weather conditions, unpredictable human behaviour and bizarre edge cases.

When Volvo introduced its semi-autonomous cars into Australia in 2017, they famously couldn't identify kangaroos. This was a potentially dangerous bug, as anyone who has run into a kangaroo on an Australian backroad will know. The problem was that the SLAM algorithm wasn't tuned to recognise and track animals that jump up and down, only those that walk and run.

Another problem (which troubles the public a lot but experts not so much) is the famous "trolley problem". What happens when a self-driving car comes around a corner and finds a mother and child in the middle of the road? Does it swerve, perhaps hitting a brick wall and killing the car's occupants? Or does it run over the pedestrians, killing them?

> The trolley problem is a philosophical dilemma introduced by the English philosopher Philippa Foot in 1967 concerning a runaway railway trolley. There are five people tied up to the tracks ahead that the trolley is heading towards. You are standing next to a lever. If you pull this lever, the trolley will switch to a siding. However, there is also one person tied to the siding. You have two options: either you do nothing, and the trolley kills the five people on the main track, or you pull the lever, diverting the trolley onto the siding, where it will kill one person. What do you do?
>
> There are many variants of the trolley problem involving fat men pushed into the path of the trolly, and organs harvested from living people without their consent to save multiple lives. Indeed, philosophers now playfully talk about "trolleyology". Foot actually proposed the trolley problem as a less controversial way of discussing the moral issues around abortion. When is it reasonable, for example, to kill an unborn child to save the life of the mother?

The trolley problem may have captured the imagination of philosophers and the public alike, but is largely irrelevant to the design of self-driving cars. The car is not understanding the world well enough to have to consider such issues. If you see a video demo of a self-driving car, the road in front of the car is painted green to indicate where the car determines there are no obstacles and it is safe to drive. And if there's no green road, the car is programmed simply to brake as hard as possible. That's it. The top-level control loop of a self-driving car is simply:

DRIVE ON THE GREEN ROAD otherwise BRAKE AS HARD AS POSSIBLE.

I imagine we will succeed in tackling the problems that keep us from Level 5 (full autonomy). At the end of the day, self-driving cars have many advantages over cars driven by humans. They have active sensors that can map the world in the dark or bad weather. They act at electronic and not biological speeds. And they won't ever be tired, distracted or drunk. If adolescent humans can do it, I have few doubts we'll get computers to drive too.

Experts have varying opinions on how long it will take to achieve Level 5 autonomy. Some optimists suggest it could be within the next five to 10 years, while others believe it might take decades. In part, how long it takes will depend on our tolerance for AI-caused harm compared to human-caused harm. But however long it takes, I expect we'll look back and marvel at the time we let humans drive cars and cause all the carnage we experience today on our roads. And, for that, we will have to thank the Reverend Thomas Bayes.

PART 3
THE FUTURE

ACHIEVING AI

"What we have now is not what will be. When it comes to AI models, what we have now will advance at a faster rate than any technology we have ever seen. One thing we can all agree on: it's a fucking weird time to be alive."
Stephen Fry, CogX Festival, September 2023

THIS BRINGS US UP the present day. You can't open a newspaper today without reading multiple stories about how AI is entering our lives. In many cases, the headlines are anxious, negative or downright hysterical.

Of course, the history of AI is still being written. While the AI systems we have today are impressive and, in some cases, a little worrying, we still have a long way to go to our ultimate goal: to match human intelligence in all its richness. I have no doubt that, over the next 10, 50 or perhaps 100 years, we'll achieve that. And, having matched human intelligence, we will likely go way past it. It would be terribly conceited to think we couldn't. After all, what's so special about human intelligence? And in narrow areas, be it playing chess or reading X-rays or predicting turbine faults, AI is already superhuman.

This is not the first time that technology has threatened to be disruptive. Other technologies – from the steam engine to electricity – have already transformed our lives dramatically. Just like these previous technologies, AI will transform every aspect of our lives: how we are born, live, work, play and die. But there is one way that the AI revolution will likely be different. And that is the speed with which it transforms our lives.

The industrial revolution took over 50 years to play out. Electricity took several decades. Even the internet took a decade or so to take hold, as we had to get people online. The AI revolution is different. We've already put in the plumbing. You only need to be told the URL or the API of some AI service and you can get to work. Vast amounts of money are being invested in AI. In 2024, around US$1 billion was invested in artificial intelligence *every day*. We've never seen anything like this scale of investment previously. And it is starting to pay off. In one year from launching ChatGPT, OpenAI went from no income to over US$1 billion per year, and a valuation of somewhere around US$100 billion.* We have never before seen such phenomenal growth in the history of capitalism. AI is arguably the largest gold rush ever. In terms of both revenue and market value, OpenAI is the fastest-growing company ever to have been founded.

---

* Despite its remarkable increase in revenues, OpenAI is still losing several billion dollars per year.

It is often said that we live in exponential times. Computers have been doubling in power every two or so years since the 1950s. This is called Moore's law. The amount of data online, vital for AI technologies like machine learning, has also been doubling in quantity every two years. And many of the fundamental AI algorithms have seen similar doublings in performance in recent years, driven by algorithmic breakthroughs like transformers.

But there's another exponential that is less talked about: science itself. Nowhere is that more apparent than in AI. The 2024 AI Index records that the number of scientific publications in AI put out each year has doubled over the last five years.[1] And, reflecting AI's increasing adoption by industry, the number of AI patents filed (and AI patents granted) annually is currently doubling every two years. You can expect, therefore, many of the limitations in current AI systems to be addressed in the near future. But if this is the case, it invites the obvious question: how is it all going to end?

THE SINGULARITY

One incredibly seductive end point for AI is the technological singularity. It's an idea that can be traced back to the beginnings of AI in the 1950s and the remarkable John von Neumann, one of the fathers of computing. He warned of "the ever accelerating progress of technology and changes in the mode of human life, which gives the appearance of approaching some essential singularity in the history of the race beyond which human affairs, as we know them, could not continue".[2] More recently, the singularity has been popularised by the science fiction author Vernor Vinge, the futurist Ray Kurzweil, the philosopher Nick Bostrom and others.

The AI singularity is the point when we have developed an AI system so intelligent that it can recursively redesign itself to be even more intelligent. This new, more intelligent, AI system would then be able to redesign itself again to be even more intelligent, creating a snowball effect. Unlike biological evolution, which takes thousands of years, this recursive improvement might happen overnight, resulting in an artificial intelligence that suddenly far exceeds human intelligence.

But why would "human affairs" not be able to continue past this point? The problem is that we would no longer be the most intelligent species on the planet. And humanity got to be the dominant species on the planet by dint of our intelligence. We weren't the fastest or the strongest animal, but we were the smartest. And we used this intelligence to invent language in order to cooperate, and tools to amplify our muscles, and this put us in charge of planet Earth. The fate of other, less intelligent, species now depends on us.

Similarly, if artificial intelligence is smarter than us, our fate might depend on the benevolence of those machines. It may not be that the machines have ill intent. If we're building a new housing estate, and an anthill happens to be in the way, we'll bulldoze the anthill. The ants aren't important enough for us to care what happens to them. And just as ants can't contain what humans do, how can we hope to contain AI that is more intelligent than us?

Let me provide a few consoling thoughts to these worrying

ideas about the coming singularity. First, we might run into a brick wall. There are fundamental limits to many physical phenomena. Albert Einstein taught us that you cannot accelerate to faster than the speed of light. Werner Heisenberg taught us that, at the quantum level, you cannot know precisely both the position and momentum of particles. Perhaps there are physical limits to intelligence? The world is uncertain and that uncertainty limits how smart you can be. It doesn't matter how intelligent you are; there's a limit to how well you can do at the casino. Indeed, the smartest thing you can possibly do is walk out!

Second, intelligent people unsurprisingly assign a lot of importance to intelligence. But our superpower was not our intelligence but our society. It was our ability to come together and work collectively that enabled us to do much more than we can do individually. Of course, intelligence helped. Without intelligence, we would not have language, and without language, we could not work together so well. It was our ability to divide problems and conquer them collectively that permitted us to be so effective. Most of us wouldn't last long alone on a desert island. Intelligence is thus not to be feared; intelligence is something that helps us survive.

Third, intelligence greater than ours already exists and hasn't caused the end of human affairs. Indeed, it is quite the opposite. Human affairs progress as well as they do today precisely because of this greater-than-human intelligence. Such intelligence is found in human institutions like corporations and governments. No *one* person knows how to build a nuclear power station. But collectively, the people working at

Westinghouse or General Electric Hitachi and their suppliers have this knowledge.

The singularity is undoubtably an interesting possibility. And we do need to entertain the idea that machines will be more intelligent than us, and consider the consequences. But it is likely far from the greatest or most immediate risk that AI poses.

THE END OF WORK

One pressing risk is the impact that AI will have on work. Sensational headlines regularly warn of technological unemployment and make dire predictions such as that AI might put half of us out of work. As ever, the reality is likely to be far more nuanced.

One of the earliest, most detailed studies in this area came out in September 2013 from the Oxford Martin School at the University of Oxford. A report summarising this research predicted that 47 per cent of jobs in the United States were under threat of automation.[3] Similar studies have since reached broadly similar conclusions for other countries. Now, there's a lot to disagree with in the Oxford report. But even if you agree with its findings, there are many reasons why you cannot conclude that half of us will be unemployed.

First, the Oxford report merely estimated the number of jobs that are *susceptible* to automation. Some of these jobs won't be automated in practice for economical, societal, technical and other reasons. For example, we can pretty much automate the job of an airline pilot today. Indeed, most of the time, a computer is flying your plane. But society is likely to continue to demand the reassurance of having a pilot on board, even if they are just reading their iPad most of the time. As a second example, the Oxford report gives a 94 per cent chance that the job of repairing bicycles can be automated. But it is likely to be very expensive and difficult to automate this job, and therefore uneconomical to do so. And I've yet to meet a roboticist who is trying to build a bicycle repair robot.

Second, we also need to consider all the new jobs that technology will create. For example, we don't employ huge numbers of people setting movable type anymore. But we do employ many more people in related digital roles – making web pages, for example. Of course, if you are a printer and your job is replaced by a machine, it helps if you're suitably educated so you can reposition yourself in one of these new industries.

Third, some of these jobs will only be partially automated, and automation will in fact enhance our ability to do the job. For example, the Oxford report gives a 63 per cent chance to the role of a geoscientist being automated. However, automation is likely to permit geoscientists to do more geoscience. Indeed, the US Department of Labor actually predicts the next decade will see a 10 per cent increase in the number of geoscientists as we seek to make more of the planet's diminishing resources.

Fourth, we also need to consider how the working week will change over the next few decades. Most countries in the developed world have seen the number of hours worked per week decrease significantly since the start of the industrial revolution. In the United States, the average working week has declined from around 60 hours to just 33. Other developed countries are even lower. German workers only work 26 hours per week. If these trends continue, we may need to create more jobs to replace these lost hours.

People forget that the weekend was an invention of the industrial revolution. Workers demanded to have Sunday off to go to church, and then to have Saturday off to rest. But, for reasons I've never understood, we stopped asking for more. There are, however, a number of studies of four-day working weeks being conducted around the world. Invariably these studies demonstrate that people are just as productive in four days of work as five – so we can pay them as much – and that people are happier. Who would have imagined?

Fifth, we need to consider changing demographics. Most developed countries have ageing populations: more of us are retired, supported by fewer and fewer people of working age. The improved productivity that AI brings may be needed just to keep our economies afloat and the retired in pensions.

It's hard, then, to predict with any certainty how many of us will really be unemployed due to AI, but it is unlikely to be half the population. Society in its current form will break down well before we get to 50 per cent unemployment. AI is nevertheless going to have a huge impact on work, and we need to start planning for and mitigating against this disruption today.

Finally, while jobs may be displaced, there's plenty of work done today that we don't yet properly recognise and reward – for example, time spent looking after the elderly, the young, people with disabilities. This is work – largely done by women – that we could perhaps afford to pay for in a future where AI is providing significant productivity gains. Now that would be a fine future!

FUTURE CHALLENGES

The future of work isn't the only issue we need worry about today. There are many other impacts that AI will have. A powerful technology like artificial intelligence is a double-edged sword. Along with the many benefits – perhaps none more important than the transformation of medicine and education – come many risks.

In August 2023, the Science, Innovation and Technology Committee of the UK House of Commons did a good job identifying some of the most important challenges posed by AI.[4]

- **The Bias challenge.** AI may create or perpetuate biases that society finds unacceptable.

- **The Privacy challenge.** AI may identify individuals or provide personal information about them beyond what the public expects.

- **The Misrepresentation challenge.** AI may generate content that misrepresents someone's behaviour, opinions or character, as well as about important issues like the climate or political parties.

- **The Access to Data challenge.** The most powerful AI systems require access to very large datasets, which are held by few organisations.

- **The Access to Compute challenge.** The most powerful AI requires access to significant amounts of computation, available to only to a few organisations.

- **The Black Box challenge.** AI models often cannot explain why they produce a particular result.

- **The Open-Source challenge.** Making AI code openly available may promote transparency and innovation but may enable bad actors to commit harm. On the other hand, making code proprietary may prevent this but may concentrate market power.

- **The Intellectual Property and Copyright challenge.** Large AI models are often trained on copyrighted content without the consent of owners or their compensation. It remains uncertain then who owns the outputs.

- **The Liability challenge.** If AI models are used by third parties and cause harm, we must establish who bears any liability.

- **The Employment challenge.** As I've discussed, AI will disrupt the jobs that people do and that are available to be done. We must manage this disruption carefully.

- **The International Coordination challenge.** AI is being developed around the world, so any governance frameworks to regulate it require international cooperation.

- **The Existential challenge.** AI might pose a threat to the human species itself.

This is a pretty worrying list of challenges. And it's not even exhaustive; I can think of several other challenges that AI poses. There's the **Environmental challenge** of large AI models producing CO_2 and consuming cooling water, as well as the **Democratic challenge** posed by AI being used to influence voters and upset elections around the world. And indeed, most of these "future challenges" are in fact also *present* challenges. For example, multiple class-action suits about intellectual property and copyright are underway in the US against companies like OpenAI. Can technology companies use vast amounts of copyrighted material to train large language models without consent or compensation? Is it fair use to do so?

It's impossible to say how such legal cases will play out. Previous lawsuits that might help set precedents have gone both ways. In 2013, Google won a class-action suit brought by the American Authors Guild that recognised the scanning and summarisation of millions of texts by Google Books as fair use. The US Supreme Court upheld this ruling in April 2016. On the other hand, Napster ceased operations in 2001 after losing multiple lawsuits about copyright infringement, despite identifying and blocking 99.4 per cent of infringing material.

One thing is clear: the road ahead will be bumpy.

When people ask me if I'm optimistic or pessimistic about the challenges that AI poses, I say that I'm both. I'm optimistic that AI will ultimately bring great benefits. But in the short term, I'm pessimistic. Sadly, our children are set to inherit a worse world than the one we were born into, due to a raft of problems, some of which are caused by AI, such as technological unemployment and distrust in the very institutions that we now need most.

The next decade or two will be challenging. Technologies like AI could help us tackle many of these problems. But to profit from AI, we will need to learn from history. Social media, for example, should have been a wake-up call for how technology can disrupt our lives. We are now about to supercharge this disruption with AI. We had better learn then from the lessons of the past.

Perhaps this book isn't a bad place to start?

IMAGE CREDITS

p. ix: Ada Lovelace: Alfred Edward Chalon [presumed], *Portrait of Ada King, Countess of Lovelace*, c. 1840. Collection of Science Museum. Image via Wikimedia Commons; Nimatron patent: Edward Condon, US Patent 2215544, 26 April 1942. Image via Wikimedia Commons; Shakey: Collection of SRI International. Image via Wikimedia Commons; Marion Tinsley: Photograph Mark T. Foley. Image via Wikimedia Commons / Florida Memory.

p. x: Stanley: Photograph by Sanao. Image via Wikimedia Commons; Watson / *Jeopardy!*: Ben Hider / Getty Images; Chinook: Unknown photographer via Hackernoon / Medium; Fei-Fei Li: Photograph by ITU / R. Farrell at AI for GOOD Global Summit. Image via Flickr, CC 2.0; Elon Musk: Photograph by Steve Jurvetson. Image via Flickr, CC 2.0; Sophia: DPA Picture Alliance / Alamy Stock Photo.

p. 4: Image courtesy of MIT Museum.

p. 13: © Bank of England.

p. 16: Alfred Edward Chalon [presumed], *Portrait of Ada King, Countess of Lovelace*, c. 1840. Collection of Science Museum. Image via Wikimedia Commons.

p. 22: Everett Collection Historical / Alamy Stock Photo.

p. 28: Collection of Berlin Zoological Garden. Image via Wikimedia Commons.

p. 32: Collection of SRI International. Image via Wikimedia Commons.

p. 34: Timothy Colburn / University of Minnesota.

p. 39: Henri de Parville, 'La tour d'Hanoï et la question du Tonkin', *La Nature*, vol. 12, no. 548, Dec 1884, pp. 285–6.

p. 49: Patent: Edward Condon, US Patent 2215544, 26 April 1942. Image via Wikimedia Commons; photograph: Unknown photographer. Image courtesy of Historic Pittsburgh.

IMAGE CREDITS

p. 56: Unknown photographer via afflictor.com, with permission of Jonathan Schaeffer.

p. 81: Public domain; image via Owen Holland, 'The first biologically inspired robots', *Robotica*, vol. 21, 2003, p. 354.

p. 91 DPA Picture Alliance / Alamy Stock Photo.

p. 98: Walter Pitts: Unknown photographer, c. 1954. Image via Wikimedia Commons; Warren McCulloch: Photograph by Lotfi A. Zadeh, reproduced courtesy of Norman Zadeh. Image via EECS Berkeley.

p. 104: George Boole: Unknown artist, c. 1864–5. Image via Haks / Wikimedia Commons; Geoff Hinton: Photograph by Ramsey Cardy / Collision Conference. Image via Sportsfile via Flickr, CC 2.0.

p. 108: Photograph by ITU / R. Farrell at AI for GOOD Global Summit. Image via Flickr, CC 2.0.

p. 119: Photograph by Steve Jennings / Getty Images for TechCrunch. Image via Flickr, CC 2.0.

p. 135: Graph by Alan Laver, based on OurWorldInData.org/artificial-intelligence, data by Epoch (2023). CC BY.

p. 139: Photograph by Matthew Scroggs. Image via Wikimedia Commons.

p. 141: Demis Hassabis: Photograph by The Royal Society / Duncan Hull. Image via Wikimedia Commons. Mustafa Suleyman: Photograph by Christopher Wilson. Image via Wikimedia Commons.

p. 148: Stan Honda / Getty Images.

p. 154: Ben Hider / Getty Images.

p. 165: From Terence O'Donnell, *History of Life Insurance in Its Formative Years*, Chicago: American Conservation Co., 1936, p. 335. Image via Wikimedia Commons.

ACKNOWLEDGEMENTS

It takes many people to write a book. I therefore want to thank a bunch of wonderful people, without whom this book would not exist, starting with Morry Schwartz and the whole team at Black Inc. They commissioned this book, so I hope they aren't regretting their decision. I enjoyed writing this book greatly, which I take to be a promising sign.

My colleagues at UNSW Sydney, CSIRO Data61 and elsewhere, especially my PhD students, postdocs and research collaborators. They provide the stimulating environment in which I continue to explore these AI dreams.

My editor, Jo Rosenberg. I'm always amazed how she can delete text to uncover a much better book!

My literary agent, Margaret Gee.

My speaking agent, Nadia Petrik, for expertly managing my public engagements, where I continue the important conversations raised in my books. You can reach her via http://tobywalsh.ai.

But above all, I want to thank my family. They generously gave me the time to write another book. They are everything to me.

NOTES

HOW IT BEGINS
1. Nestor Maslej et al., 2024, *Artificial Intelligence Index Report 2024*, Stanford: Institute for Human-Centered AI, Stanford University.
2. Arthur L. Samuel, 1962, "Artificial Intelligence: A Frontier of Automation", *The Annals of the American Academy of Political and Social Science* 340 (1), pp. 10–20.
3. A.M. Turing, 1950, "Computing Machinery and Intelligence", *Mind* 59 (236), pp. 433–60.
4. Ada Lovelace, 1843, "Note A. Sketch of the Analytical Engine Invented by Charles Babbage, Esq. By L.F. Menabrea of Turin, Officer of the Military Engineers", *Scientific Memoirs* 3.
5. Ada Lovelace, 1843, "Note G. Sketch of the Analytical Engine Invented by Charles Babbage, Esq. By L.F. Menabrea of Turin, Officer of the Military Engineers", *Scientific Memoirs* 3.
6. Thomas Hobbes, 1655, *De Corpore*, in *The Collected Works of Thomas Hobbes*, edited by Sir William Molesworth, London: Routledge Themes Press, 1992.

PART 1: THE SYMBOLIC ERA

IDEA #1: SEARCHING FOR ANSWERS
1. John Searle, 1999, "The Chinese Room", in *The MIT Encyclopedia of the Cognitive Sciences*, edited by R.A. Wilson and F. Keil, Cambridge, MA: MIT Press.
2. P.E. Hart, N.J. Nilsson and B. Raphael, 1968, "A Formal Basis for the Heuristic Determination of Minimum Cost Paths", *IEEE Transactions on Systems Science and Cybernetics* 4 (2), pp. 100–7.

3. Herbert A. Simon, 1947, *Administrative Behavior: A Study of Decision-Making Processes in Administrative Organization*, New York: Macmillan, p. 82.
4. Pamela McCorduck, 2004, *Machines Who Think*, 2nd ed., Natick: A.K. Peters, Ltd.
5. Quoted in Daniel Crevier, 1993, *AI: The Tumultuous Search for Artificial Intelligence*, New York: Basic Books.
6. Richard E. Fikes and Nils J. Nilsson, 1971, "STRIPS: A New Approach to the Application of Theorem Proving to Problem Solving", *Artificial Intelligence* 2 (3–4), pp. 189–208.

IDEA #2: MAKING THE BEST MOVE
1. Gereld L. Tawney and Willard A. Derr, "Machine to Play Game of Nim", U.S. Patent Number 2,215,544.
2. Garry Kasparov, 1996, "The Day That I Sensed a New Kind of Intelligence", *Time*, March 25.
3. *San Francisco Chronicle*, 1990, "Robot Whips Backgammon Champ", 17 July, p. 1.
4. J. Schaeffer et al., 2007, "Checkers Is Solved", *Science* 317 (5844), pp. 1518–22.
5. References to these perfect solutions:
    Nim: C.L. Bouton, 1901–02, "Nim, A Game with a Complete Mathematical Theory", *Annals of Mathematics* 3 (14), pp. 35–39.
    Connect 4: "John's Connect Four Playground", John Tromp, accessed August 2024, https://tromp.github.io/c4/c4.html.
    Othello: Hiroki Takizawa, 2024, "Othello Is Solved", *arXiv*, 2 January, https://arxiv.org/abs/2310.19387.
    Tic-Tac-Toe: "Complete Map of Optimal Tic-Tac-Toe Positions", XKCD, accessed August 2024, https://xkcd.com/832.
6. Cade Metz, 2017, "Artificial Intelligence Is About to Conquer Poker – But Not Without Human Help", *Wired*, January 24.
7. Malcolm Gladwell, 2008, *Outliers: The Story of Success*, New York: Little, Brown and Co.

INTERMISSION

THE ROBOTS ARE COMING
1. Hans Moravec, 1988, *Mind Children: The Future of Robot and Human Intelligence*, Cambridge, MA: Harvard University Press, p. 15.
2. Steven Pinker, 1994, *The Language Instinct: How the Mind Creates Language*, New York: HarperCollins.
3. "Unimate Robot", YouTube, accessed August 2024, https://tinyurl.com/UnimateRobot.

NOTES

IDEA #4: ARTIFICIAL BRAINS
1. "New Navy Device Learns by Doing", *New York Times*, 9 July 1958.
2. Quoted in Melanie Lefkowitz, 2019, "Professor's Perceptron Paved the Way for AI – 60 Years Too Soon", *Cornell Chronicle*, 25 September.
3. Jürgen Schmidhuber, 2012, "Multi-Column Deep Neural Networks for Image Classification", in *Proceedings of the 2012 IEEE Conference on Computer Vision and Pattern Recognition*, Washington, D.C.: IEEE Computer Society, pp. 3642–49.
4. Ashish Vaswani et al, 2017, "Attention Is All you Need", *NIPS '17 Advances in Neural Information Processing Systems* 30, pp. 6000–10.
5. Tolga Bolukbasi et al., 2016, "Man Is to Computer Programmer as Woman Is to Homemaker? Debiasing Word Embeddings", *Proceedings of the 30th International Conference on Neural Information Processing Systems (NIPS 2016)*, pp. 4356–64.
6. Jacob Devlin et al., 2019, "BERT: Pre-Training of Deep Bidirectional Transformers for Language Understanding", in *Proceedings of the 2019 Conference of the North American Chapter of the Association for Computational Linguistics: Human Language Technologies*, Minneapolis: Association for Computational Linguistics, pp. 4171–86.

IDEA #5: REWARDING SUCCESS
1. European Molecular Biology Laboratory's European Bioinformatics Institute, 2023, EMBL-EBI Highlights, available online.

IDEA #6: REASONING ABOUT BELIEFS
1. Harold Jeffreys, 1973, *Scientific Inference*, 3rd ed., Cambridge: Cambridge University Press, p. 31.
2. Libby Plummer, 2017, "This Is How Netflix's Top-Secret Recommendation System Works", *Wired*, August 22.
3. John Davies, 1990, *A History of Wales*, London: Penguin.

PART 3: THE FUTURE

ACHIEVING AI
1. Maslej et al., Artificial Intelligence Index Report 2024.
2. Stanislaw Ulam, 1958, "Tribute to John von Neumann", *Bulletin of the American Mathematical Society* 64 (3, Part 2).
3. Carl Benedikt Frey and Michael A. Osborne, 2013, "The Future of Employment: How Susceptible Are Jobs to Computerisation?", research paper, 17 September, https://tinyurl.com/FutureOfWork2013.
4. House of Commons Science, Innovation and Technology Committee, 2023, *The Governance of Artificial Intelligence: Interim Report*, 31 August.

INDEX

Page references in **bold** are to illustrations.

8-puzzle 34–5
21 (game) 45–7
2001: A Space Odyssey (movie) 23, 52, 70, 83–4
2062: The World that AI Made (book) x

A* search (algorithm) ix, 31–3
Adams, Douglas 1, 84–5
Addams Family (TV series) 10
Advanced Micro Devices 69
AGI (artificial general intelligence) x, 124, 142
agriculture 76, 152
AI. *See* artificial intelligence
AI spring x
AI winter ix, x, 61–2, 66
Alexa 70
AlexNet (deep learning neural network) x, 109–10, 111
algorithms ix, 76
    bias in 129
    learning 107
    performance of 61, 177
    SLAM 169
    vision 109, 159
    See also A* search; Minimax
Allen AI 118
AlphaFold x, 151–2
    See also DeepMind

AlphaGo x, 144–9
    See also DeepMind
Altman, Sam x, **119**–120, 123, 132
    See also OpenAI
Alvey program 69
Alzheimer's disease 23
Amazon 87
    Mechanical Turk 108
American Authors Guild 185
analogue electronics 81–2
Analytical Engine ix, 15–18
    See also Lovelace, Ada
Angle, Colin 86n
antibiotics 22–3
archaeology 86
Aristotle 27–8, 37
artificial general intelligence (AGI) x, 124, 142
artificial intelligence
    acceleration of 176–7
    in antiquity 20–3
    biases in 117, 126, 129, 131, 183
    coining of term ix, 6
    criticism of 18
    economics of 144–6
    environmental harm caused by 185
    existential threat posed by 8, 185
    fear of 8, 175, 178, 185
    funding for 144–6

195

INDEX

artificial intelligence (*cont.*)
    and gender 3, 90–2, 116–17
    generations of 68–9
    investment in 176
    invisibility of 2
    liability for harm by 184
    origins of 1–3
    pessimism about 186
    in popular culture 9–11
    prehistory of 11–20, 106
    regulation and coordination of 185
    ubiquity of 71
    unintended consequences of 21–2, 22, 129, 177–8, 183–6
Asimov, Isaac 2
Athens 27–8
Austin, Texas 69, 70
Australian Computer Society 50
auto-complete 126–7
automatic collision avoidance 76, 89–90
autonomous vehicles. *See* cars, self-driving
aviation 13, 30, 70, 180

Babbage, Charles ix, 15–18
backgammon ix, 54–5
backpropagation 102, 105–7, 109
BackRub 4–5
    See also Google
Bacon, Francis 64
Baggini, Julian 130
Baidu 110, 118
Bayes, Thomas 159–60, 164–5, 171
Bayes' theorem 159–64
    and SLAM 166–71
Bel Geddes, Norman 87
Bell Labs 109
Bennett, John Makepeace 50
Berliner, Hans 54
Bernoulli numbers 17
BERT (AI system) 118–19, 121
Bing 124
biology 150–2, 178
bio-machines 79–80
biotechnology 152
BKG 9.8 ix, 54–5
Blade Runner (movie) 10
Bletchley Park 51, 140
    See also Turing, Alan

boats, robotic 76
bomb defusing 86
Bombe 12
Boole, George 19, 67, 103–4
Boolean logic 19, 48, 103
Bostrom, Nick 178
Bowling, Michael 58
brain, artificial 38, 75, 80, 95–100
    See also neural networks; perceptrons; robots and robotics
brain, human 97, 101, 166
    capability of 51, 55
    diseases of 23
    evolution of 79
    structure of 112
Brain Bar (Budapest) 91
Bristol, UK ix, 81
Brockman, Greg 119
Bronx High School of Science 103
Brooks, Rodney 77, 85–6, 130
Brown, Gordon 15
Bryson, Arthur E. 106
Buchanan, Bruce 65
Bundy, Alan 12n
Burden Neurological Institute 81
business rules 70–1
Byron, Lord 15

C-3PO (robot) 32
calculus 19, 169
Caltech 108
Canadian Institute for Advanced Research (CIFAR) 105
Čapek, Karel 79–80
Carnegie Group 66
Carnegie Mellon University (formerly Carnegie Institute of Technology) 31–2, 35, 54, 59, 89, 105
cars, self-driving **x**, 4, 87–90, 107
    autonomy of 166–71
    benefits of 167, 170
    by Volvo 168
    See also Stanley
Carson, Johnny 82
Cepheus (AI bot) 58
Champernowne, David ix, 36, 51
chance, games of 58
    See also games
Charles II, King 19

INDEX

chatbots
    capabilities of 78
    first example of ix
    as therapists 135
    training of 122
    See also ChatGPT; ELIZA; ERNIE
ChatGPT 8, 78, 110, 124–32
    coining of name of x, 123, 124
    and *Jeopardy!* 154–5
    launch of (2022) x, 2, 124–5, 176
    limitations of 43–4, 127–32
    and questions 114
    and reinforcement learning 156–8
    and transformers 113
    See also OpenAI
checkers x, 8, 36, 56–7, 77
chemistry 65
cheques, reading of 109–10
chess ix, x, 7, 36, 51–5
    and Demis Hassabis 141
    enjoyment of 149
    invention of 42–3
    learning of 137–8, 149
    strategy for 45–8, 146–7
    See also Deep Blue; Stockfish; Turochamp
China 27, 28, 108
    and AI competition 144–5
    games in 49, 144
    and surveillance 10
Chinese room argument 29–30
Chinook (checkers program) x, **56**–7
Clarke, Arthur C. ix, 1–2, 83–4
climate change 22, 183
codebreaking 12, 51, 140
Cold War 62, 144
competition, international 144–6
computer vision 75–6, 89, 105, 107–11, 159
computer-aided design 69
computers
    abilities and limitations of 12–14, 18, 29–30, 55, 59–60, 66–7 (*See also* Turing, Alan)
    and creativity ix, 18, 37
    human 17
    power of 184
Connect-4 57
contraceptive pill 64
Control Data 69

copyright 122, 184, 185
Cornell University 100
Covid-19 43, 160–4
credit assignment 138–9
crime-fighting 76
Cruise 90
cryptocurrency 21
cyborgs 10
cyclones, prediction of 23

DALL-E 114
Dalle Molle Institute for Artificial Intelligence (Switzerland) 142
DanNet 110
DARPA (Defense Advanced Research Projects Agency) 62, 69
DARPA Prize x, 4, 88–9, 167
Dartmouth College, 1956 meeting at ix, 3, 6–8, 11, 15, 27, 35, 48, 101
data
    control over 183
    quantities of 177, 185
    sequential 111–14
    training 107–9, 121–2, 131, 135–6, 185
databases
    management of 69
    of proteins 152
DEC 69
decision-making 31–2, 35–6, 55, 70, 87
decoding 118
Deep Blue (IBM chess computer) x, 52–3, 146–8, 152
deep learning x, 96, 103–11, 126
    See also backpropagation
DeepMind x, 11, 110, 121
    founding of 141–3
    and protein structure 150–2
    See also AlphaFold; AlphaGo
Deepwater Horizon disaster 87
defence systems 10, 11
democracy 22, 185
demography 182
DENDRAL (expert system) ix, 64–5
Descript 113
disinformation 22, 118, 128
Djerassi, Carl 64
DNNResearch 110
Dota 2 (game) 120–1
draughts. *See* checkers

197

INDEX

Einstein, Albert 179
Eliot, T.S. 36
ELIZA (chatbot) ix, 133–5
Elmer and Elsie (robots) ix, 80–2, **81**
ELMo (encoder) 118
email 159, 164
emotions 10, 79, 80, 85
encoding 63–5, 116–18
Engelberger, Joseph 82–3
Engine, Analytical ix, 15–18
Enigma code 12
ERNIE (chatbot) 118
European Bioinformatics Institute 152
European Union 89
Everest, George 19, 103–4
Everest, Mary 19
evolution, and intelligence 79
Ex Machina (movie) 10–11
expert systems ix, x, 62–7, 70
expertise
    nature of 66
    simulation of 63, 65, 67
exponential explosion 40, 42–3

Facebook 86, 92, 131
    See also Meta
Fallon, Jimmy 91
feedback, human 156–8
Feigenbaum, Edward 64–5
Fermat's Last Theorem 12
Ferranti 50
Festival of Britain 1951 50
Fifth Generation Systems x, 68–9
financial systems 11
Flinders University 85
Foot, Philippa 169
Forbidden Planet (movie) 10
Frankenstein, or the Modern Prometheus (book) 21–2
fraud detection 23
Fry, Stephen 175
Fukushima nuclear disaster 87
fuzzy logic 98

Galactica 131
games ix, 7
    of chance 58
    and DeepMind 143
    first using AI 49–51, 59–60
    perfection at 57
    and strategy 45–8
    See also 8-puzzle; 21; backgammon; checkers; chess; Dota 2; Go; *Jeopardy!*; Nim; Nimatron; noughts and crosses; poker; *Theme Park*
Gardner, Howard 48
Gatsby Computational Neuroscience Unit 142
Gemini 110
General Language Understanding Evaluation (GLUE benchmark) 123
General Motors 82
general purpose technology 118, 124
Generative Pre-trained Transformer (GPT) 123–4
Go (Chinese game) 144–7
Go (game) x
Golem 21, 79
Goodstein, Reuben 12n
Goodstein's theorem 12n
Google 110–11, 141
    and AlphaGo 147
    and BERT 118
    Books 185
    Cloud 108
    and DeepMind 143
    origins and naming of 4–5
    Research x, 112–13
    Translate 113
googol 5
GPS 33, 166–71
GPT-1, GPT-2, GPT-3, GPT-4 121–3, 135–6, 156
GPT (Generative Pre-trained Transformer) 123–4
GPU (graphics processing unit) 106, 109–10, 136
Greek mythology and culture 21, 27–9, 37
Greiner, Helen 86n
grounding, of symbols 29, 30
GROVER (fake-news detector) 118

HAL 9000 (fictional robot) 32, 70, 83–4
Halicin (antibiotic) 22–3
hallucination 128–32
Hannan, Daniel 36
Hanson Jr, David 90–1
Hanson Robotics 90–2

INDEX

Harvard University 48
Hassabis, Demis x, **141**–142
Hauer, Rutger 10
Heisenberg, Werner 179
Hephaestus 21
Hinton, Geoffrey Everest x, 103–10, **104**, 115
hippocampus 166
Hitchhiker's Guide to the Galaxy 1, 84–5
Hobbes, Thomas 19–20, 64
Hoffman, Reid 120
Honeywell 69
Hopfield, John x
human feedback 156–8
human intelligence 178–9
human interfaces 69
Hunt, Ethan 11
Hunterian Museum, London 15

IBM x, 71, 84
    650 mainframe computer 3
    704 computer 100
    monetary value of 152
    RS/6000 supercomputer 52
    See also Deep Blue; Watson
image recognition x, 111
    See also ImageNet
ImageNet x, 107–9
ImageNet Large Scale Visual Recognition Challenge 109
IMF (International Monetary Fund) 11
Imperial College 11
income inequality 22
India 28, 40
    and chess 42–3
inequality 22
Inference Corporation 66
InRule Technology 71
intellectual property 122, 145, 177, 184, 185
Intellicorp 66
intelligence, human 178–9
interfaces, human 69
International Monetary Fund (IMF) 11
International Panic Day 1
International Space Station 70
intuition 43, 66
iRobot x, 85–7

Jacquard loom 16, 18

Japan x, 68–9, 87
Jennings, Ken 153–5, **154**
Jeopardy! **x**, 152–6
Johansson, Scarlett 9
Jumper, John x

Kashi Vishwanath 40
Kasparov, Garry x, 52–4, 146–9, **148**
Kelley, Henry J. 106
Kendrew, John 150
Kim, Dong 59
King's College, Cambridge 51
knowledge acquisition bottleneck 66
"Knowledge is power!" 64
Knut (polar bear) 27–**8**, 29
Krizhevsky, Alex 106, 109–11
Kubrick, Stanley 52, 84, 89
Kurzweil, Ray 178

Lafferty, Don 56
Lang, Fritz 9
language
    and the human brain 112
    relationships in 115–18
    and symbols 29–30
Lanier, Jaron 130
large language models 121
    limitations of 127–9
    and reinforcement learning 156–8
    and scaling 135–6
    See also ChatGPT
learning 7, 95–6
    machines 95–6
    See also deep learning; machine learning; reinforcement learning
LeCun, Yann 91–2, 109, 131
Lederberg, Joshua 64
Legg, Shane 141–2
Leibniz, Gottfried Wilhelm 19, 99, 106
LeNet-5 109
Leviathan (book) 64
Li, Fei-Fei **x**, 107–**8**
Libratus (poker program) x, 58–60
lidar 88, 166, 167
Lighthill, James ix, 61
Linnainmaa, Seppo 106
Livingstone, Ken 142
Llull, Ramon 20
logic programming 67–8, 70

INDEX

Logic Theorist (computer program) ix, 35–8
Logicians, Chinese 28
Lovelace, Ada ix, 15–18, **16**, 30, 60
Lucas, Édouard 40

machine learning 7, 8, 60, 66, 95–6, 102, 107, 177
mail, sorting of 110
Man vs. Machine World Checkers Championship 56
maps and mapping x, 31–5, 86, 166–71
Mark 1 Perceptron 100–1
Marvin (fictional robot) 84–5
mass spectrometry 65
matchbox computer 138–9
mathematicians, artificial ix, 33–8
mathematics
    foundations of 36–7
    theory of 97, 99
MCC (Microelectronics and Computer Corporation) 69
McCarthy, John ix, 3–7, **4**, 102
McCorduck, Pamela 37
McCulloch, Warren ix, 97–9, **98**
medicine 22–3, 62, 65, 152
Meditationes Sacrae (book) 64
MENACE (Machine Educable Noughts and Crosses Engine) ix, 138–**9**
Meta 109, 111
    and Galactica 131
    See also Facebook
meteorology 23, 111, 168, 170
Metropolis (movie) 9
Michie, Donald ix, 138–40
Microelectronics and Computer Corporation (MCC) 69
microprocessors 68, 69
Microsoft 69, 110, 141
    and Bing 124
    and OpenAI 120
mind–body problem 38
Minimax (algorithm) 46–7, 51
Minos 21
Minsky, Marvin 77, 101–3
misinformation 22, 128, 157, 183
Mission Impossible: Dead Reckoning (movie) 11
MIT (Massachusetts Institute of Technology) ix, 85–6, 101, 133
modus tollens law 36–7
Moore's law 102, 177
Moravec, Hans 77
Moravec's paradox 76–9
motion planning 75
Motorola 69
movies 9–11, 31, 164
music 17–18, 30, 103, 111, 145
Musk, Elon 87–8
    and OpenAI **x**, 11, 119–20
    and self-driving cars 168
    and Tesla 2
    in *Transcendence* 11
Muslim Youth Helpline 142
mythology, ancient 20–1, 40

Napster 185
NASA 83
National Air and Space Museum (Washington, D.C.) 89
National Research Council (USA) 62
National Semiconductor 69
navigation 31–3, 35, 86, 90
    See also cars, self-driving; GPS; maps and mapping
NCR 109
Neeson, Liam 60
Netflix 164
networks, neural. *See* neural networks
neural networks ix, 82, 100
    convolutional 112
    deep 106–10
    and images x
    opposition to 104
    and probabilities 159–64
    scaling of 135–6
    See also AlexNet; DanNet; DNNResearch; GPU; Hinton, Geoffrey Everest; large language models; LeCun, Yann; transformers
neurons, artificial 97, 99–103, 105
    See also neural networks
New York University 109
New York World's Fair ix, 49
Newell, Allen 35–6
Newton, Isaac 19, 135, 165
Nim (game) 49–50, 57

INDEX

Nimatron ix, **49–50**
Nimrod 50
Nobel Prize x, 35, 64, 103, 150
noughts and crosses ix, 57, 138–9
nuclear power 43, 65, 87, 179
nuclear weapons 22, 164
NVIDIA Corporation 106–7
Nyāya Sūtras 28

object recognition 107–8
OpenAI x, 110, 111, 118–24
    and copyright 185
    founding of 11, 119–20
    monetary value of 125, 176
    and movies 9
    See also Altman, Sam; ChatGPT; Musk, Elon
open-source code 151, 184
Oracle 71
Othello (Reversi) 57
Oxford Martin School 180

panic 1–2
Papert, Seymour 101, 103
parallel processing 69
patents **49**, 110, 145, 177
pathology 65
perceptrons ix, 99–102, 105–6
phototaxis 81
Pinker, Steven 77–8
Pitts, Walter ix, 97–9, **98**
Pittsburgh Supercomputing Center 59
poker x, 58–60
Pontryagin, Lev 106
Price, Richard 165
Princeton University 108
Principia Mathematica (by Whitehead and Russell) 36–7, 97, 99
privacy 183
probability 155, 159–65
PROLOG 67–8, 70
Prometheus (mythological figure) 21–2
PROMETHEUS (self-driving car) x, 89
proteins, structure of 150–2
psychotherapy 133–5
puzzles 33–4, 38–42

quantum physics 179
Queen's College, Cork 19, 104

quiz games x, 152
    See also Jeopardy!

R2-D2 (robot) 32, 79
RAND Corporation 35
reinforcement learning 120–1, 137–40
    and AlphaFold 151
    and AlphaGo 147
    and ChatGPT 125, 156–8
    from human feedback (RLHF) 156–8
    and *Jeopardy!* 153
    and Watson 153
replicants 10
Robby the Robot 10, 32
robots and robotics
    analogue 81–2
    biological 79–80
    characteristics of 75, 87
    digital 82
    domestic 76, 78–9 (*See also* Roomba)
    early examples of ix, 31–2, 79–85
    humanoid 90–2
    industrial 75, 82–3
    learning by 140
    limitations of 76–9
    in manufacturing 75, 77, 82–3
    maritime 76
    in movies 9–11, 32
    and OpenAI 121
    origin of name of 79
    rebellion by 79–80
    in space 83–5
    and unemployment 79–80
    and warfare 22
    See also cars, self-driving; Shakey the robot
Rockefeller Foundation 6
Roomba (vacuum cleaner) x, 85–7
Rosenblatt, Frank ix, 100–3, 106
Royal College of Surgeons 15
Rumelhart, David 105
R.U.R. (play) 79–80
Russell, Bertrand 36, 97–8
Russell, Stuart 143
Rutter, Brad 153–5, **154**

Safe Superintelligence 119
Samuel, Arthur 8–9, 36, 38
Sandholm, Tuomas 58

INDEX

Sandstorm (self-driving car) 89
satellites 89n, 113, 144
Saudi Arabia 90
Scale AI 86
scaling laws 135–6
Schaeffer, Jonathan 56
Schmidhuber, Jürgen 110
science fiction 2, 9–11, 21–2, 79–80, 100
Science Museum, London 15
Scroggs, Matthew **139**
Searle, John 29–30
Second World War 12, 51, 96, 133
Sedol, Lee x, 147–9
self-driving cars. *See* cars, self-driving
semiconductor packaging 69
sensing, reasoning and acting 15
sensor fusion 75
Sesame Street 118
Shakespeare, William 43, 125–6, 132
Shakey the robot ix, 31–3, **32**, 35, 40, 61, 75
 See also STRIPS (Stanford Research Institute Problem Solver)
Shanahan, Murray 11
Shane, Janelle 129–30
Shannon, Claude 48, 67
Shannon Number 48
Shelley, Mary 21–2, **22**
silicon circuits 68
Silicon Glen (Scotland) 70
Silicon Valley 5, 120
Simon, Herbert 35–6, 37
simultaneous localisation and mapping (SLAM) x, 166–71
singularity, technological 177–80
Siri 70
Skynet 10
Skype 124
SLAM (simultaneous localisation and mapping) x, 166–71
smartphones 12, 18, 30
Snapchat 124
Socrates 27, 29, 68
Sophia (robot) **x**, 90–2, **91**
space exploration 2, 65, 70, 83–5, 144
SpaceX 2
Sparkling Logic 71
speech recognition 62, 102, 114, 164
Sperry-Univac 69
spring, AI x

Sputnik 144
Square 111
Stanford AI Index 5
Stanford Artificial Intelligence Lab 108
Stanford Research Institute ix, 31, 38
 See also STRIPS
Stanford University ix, x, 4, 64, 85
 See also DENDRAL; Stanley (self-driving car)
Stanley (self-driving car) **x**, 4, 87–90, 167–71
Star Wars (movies) 32
Stockfish (chess computer) 53
Strategic Computing Initiative (of DARPA) 69
STRIPS (Stanford Research Institute Problem Solver) ix, 38–42
Suleyman, Mustafa **141**–142
supercomputers 11, 12, 16, 52, 59, 68, 154
surveillance
 in China 10
 by Roomba vacuum cleaner 86
Sutskever, Ilya 109–11, 119–20
syllogisms 27, 28
symbolic systems 7, 27–33, 102
symbols 7
 grounding of 29, 30
 manipulation of 30–1

Talos 21
Teknowledge 66
telephony 30
Terminator (movie) 10
Tesla 2, 90, 119
Theme Park (game) 142
Theophrastus 37
Thiel, Peter 120
thinking, definition of 14, 38, 82
Thornton, Janet 152
Thrun, Sebastian 89
tic-tac-toe. *See* noughts and crosses
Tinsley, Marion 56–7
Tobermory 102
tokenisation 114–17
Tonight Show 82–3, 91
Toronto Book Corpus 121–2
Tower of Hanoi puzzle 38–42, **39**
training data. *See* data: training
Transcendence (movie) 11

202

INDEX

Transformer (neural network) x
transformers 111–17
transistors 68
translation (of languages) 62, 113, 118, 123–4
trolley problem 169–70
Turing, Alan 8, 12–15, **13**, 52, 81
    at Bletchley Park 140
    and chess ix, 36, 140 (*See also* Turochamp)
    and learning machines 95–6
Turing Award 103
Turing machine 13–14, 16, 50
Turing test ix, 14, 29
Turochamp (chess computer) ix, 36, 51–2

uncertainty 58–60, 64, 159
unemployment 22, 77–80, 180–4, 186
Unimate (robot) 82
University College Cork 19n, 104
University College London 141, 142
University of Alberta 56, 58
University of California San Diego 105
University of Cambridge 12n, 51, 97, 104, 142
University of Chicago 98
University of Edinburgh ix, 12n, 105, 138, 165
University of Illinois 98
University of Oxford 142, 180
University of Toronto 105
US Postal Service 110

vacuum cleaners x, 85–7
vacuum tubes 68
VaMP (self-driving car) 89
vectors, word 115–18
Villa, Luigi ix, 54–5
Vinge, Vernor 178
vision. *See* computer vision

VITA-2 (self-driving car) 89
voice-cloning 9, 113
Volkswagen 89
von Neumann, John 177

Walsh, Toby
    life and career of 2, 19n, 66, 84, 85n
    and McCarthy, John 5
    PhD studies of 12n, 105n
Walter, William Grey ix, 81–2
warfare 22
    See also Second World War
Watson, Thomas J. 152
Watson (IBM program) x, 152–6
Waymo 90, 166
Webmind 142
Weizenbaum, Joseph ix, 133–4
Werbos, Paul 106
Westinghouse Electric Corporation 49
WhatsApp 124
Whitehead, Alfred 36, 97
Williams, Ronald J. 105
winter, AI ix, x, 61, 66
Wittgenstein, Ludwig 12n
word vectors 115–18
work, changes to 180–3
    See also unemployment
World War II. *See* Second World War
Wright brothers 13–14

xAI 119
Xi Jinping 145

Y Combinator 120

Zadeh, Lotfi 98
Zhou dynasty (China) 28
zip codes 110
Zoom 113, 114

Life is short; history is long.

The Shortest History of
INDIA
JOHN
ZUBRZYCKI

JAMES HENEAGE
The Shortest History of
GREECE

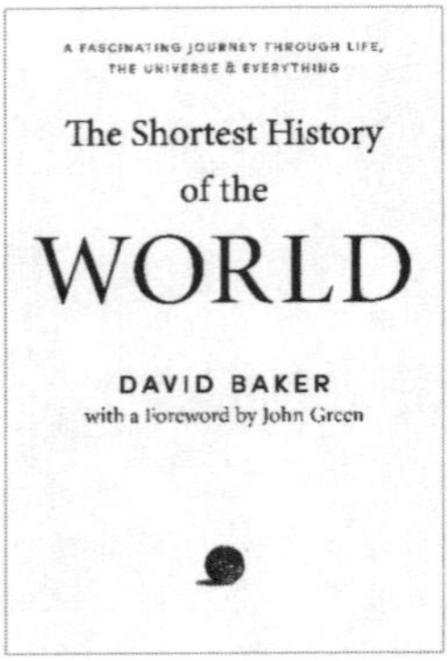
A FASCINATING JOURNEY THROUGH LIFE,
THE UNIVERSE & EVERYTHING
The Shortest History
of the
WORLD
DAVID BAKER
with a Foreword by John Green

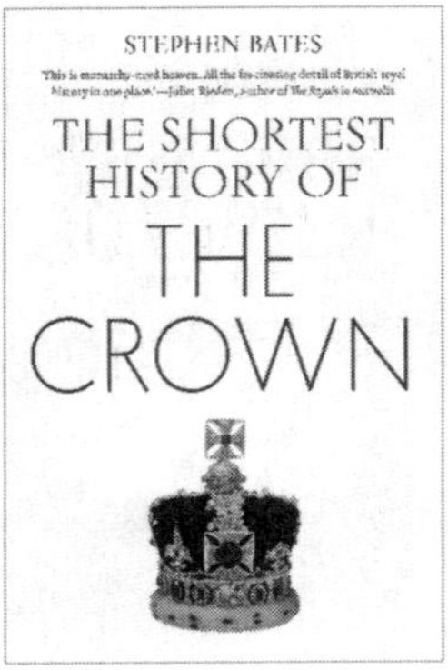
STEPHEN BATES
THE SHORTEST
HISTORY OF
THE
CROWN

THE
SHORTEST
HISTORY OF
ECONOMICS
'If you read just one book
about economics, make it
Andrew Leigh's clear, insightful
and remarkable (and short) work.'
—Professor Claudia Goldin,
Nobel Laureate in Economics,
Harvard University
ANDREW LEIGH

THE
SHORTEST
HISTORY
OF
ITALY
ROSS KING

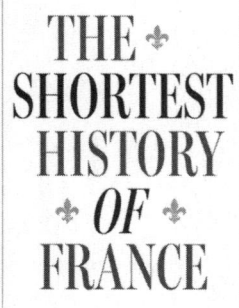

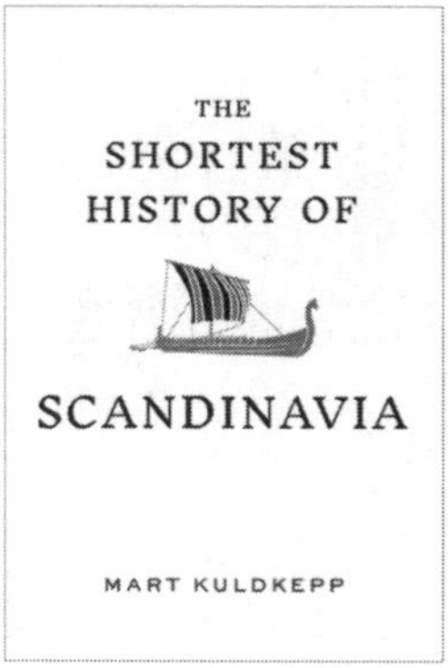

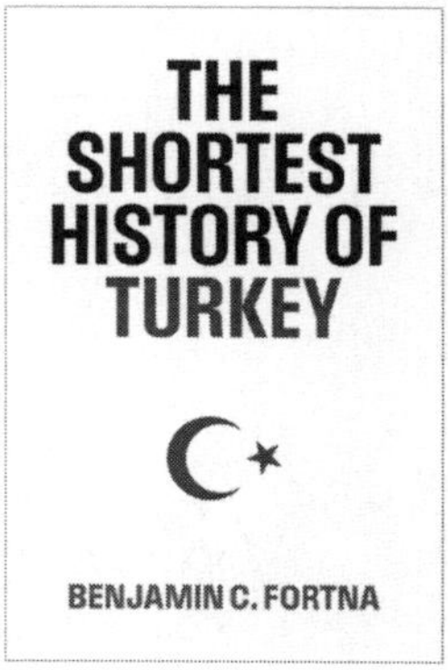

Explore the series
blackincbooks.com.au/series/shortest-history